# Doris Lessing

was born of British parents in Persia (now Iran) in 1919 and was taken to Southern Rhodesia (now Zimbabwe) when she was five. She spent her childhood on a large farm there and first came to England in 1949. She brought with her the manuscript for her first novel, *The Grass is Singing*, which was published in 1950 with outstanding success in Britain, in America, and in ten European countries. Since then her international reputation not only as a novelist but as a non-fiction and short story writer has flourished. For her collection of short novels, *Five*, she was honoured with the 1954 Somerset Maugham Award. She was awarded the Austrian State Prize for European Literature in 1981, and the German Federal Republic Shakespeare Prize of 1982. Among her other celebrated novels are *The Golden Notebook*, *The Summer Before the Dark*, *Memoirs of a Survivor* and the five volume *Children of Violence* series. Her short stories have been collected in a number of volumes, including *To Room Nineteen* and *The Temptation of Jack Orkney*, while her African stories appear in *This Was the Old Chief's Country* and *The Sun Between Their Feet*. *Shikasta*, the first in a series of five novels with the overall title of *Canopus in Argos: Archives* was published in 1979. Her novel *The Good Terrorist* won the W. H. Smith Literary Award for 1985, and the Mondello Prize in Italy that year. *The Fifth Child* won the Grinzane Cavour Prize in Italy, an award voted on by students in their final year at school. *The Making of the Representative for Planet 8* was made into an opera with Philip Glass, libretto by the author, and premièred in Houston. Her most recent works include the first volume of her autobiography, *Under My Skin*, and the novel *Love, Again*.

By the same author

# Play with a Tiger
# and Other Plays

**Flamingo**
*An Imprint of HarperCollinsPublishers*

Flamingo
An Imprint of Harp
77–85 Fulham Palace Road,
Hammersmith, London w6 8jb

Published by Flamingo 1966
9 8 7 6 5 4 3 2 1

*Each His Own Wilderness* © 1959 Doris Lessing
*Play with a Tiger* © 1962 Doris Lessing Productions Ltd
*The Singing Door* © 1973 Doris Lessing

This Collection © 1996 Doris Lessing

The Author asserts the moral right to
be identified as the author of this work

Author photograph by Caroline Forbes

ISBN 0 00 649867 1

Set in Bembo by
Rowland Phototypesetting Ltd,
Bury St Edmunds, Suffolk

Printed in Great Britain by
Caledonian International Book Manufacturing Ltd, Glasgow

# *Author's Note*

After the Second World War there was a generation uninterested in politics, even hostile to them – or at best apathetic. This troubled some of its elders, for we were passionately political. *Each His Own Wilderness* came out of watching the conflicts, listening to the arguments, between a political mother and her unpolitical son.

Soon, everything changed with the advent of the Campaign for Nuclear Disarmament, and the New Left. Youth became political, while their parents, their hearts broken by the failure of communism, drifted away from politics. The son I had watched argue with his mother for his lack of social conscience decided he had become as narrowly dogmatic as she had been, and complained she was cynical. This play is put on from time to time in Europe, and sometimes here.

*Play With a Tiger* ran at the Comedy Theatre for two months, but just under its break-even point. The reviews were mixed, not of the kind to fill the theatre. Some critics liked it. People who saw it still tell me they remember it, using adjectives like upsetting, troubling, disquieting. I wonder how it would strike young people now, for we have all become used to crueller, bleaker plays. It is sometimes put on in Europe and by small companies in the States.

*The Singing Door* was written because I was asked to do a play to be acted by children. That means a large cast, a strong story, and simple scenery that doesn't cost too much. I have not seen this play put on myself but I am told it is effective.

Doris Lessing
July 1996

# PLAY WITH A TIGER

This play was first produced at the Comedy Theatre, London, on 22 March 1962, by Oscar Lewenstein, with the following cast:

| | |
|---|---|
| ANNA FREEMAN | Siobhan McKenna |
| TOM LATTIMER | William Russell |
| MARY JACKSON | Maureen Pryor |
| HARRY PAINE | Godfrey Quigley |
| JANET STEVENS | Anne Lawson |
| DAVE MILLER | Alex Viespi |

Directed by Ted Kotcheff

The action takes place in Anna Freeman's room on the first floor of Mary Jackson's house in Earls Court, London, SW5

At the opening of the play the time is about nine in the evening; at its close it is about four in the morning

# Author's Notes on Directing this Play

When I wrote *Play with a Tiger* in 1958 I set myself an artistic problem which resulted from my decision that naturalism, or, if you like, realism, is the greatest enemy of the theatre; and that I never wanted to write a naturalistic play again.

Now this play is about the rootless, declassed people who live in bed-sitting-rooms or small flats or the cheaper hotel rooms, and such people are usually presented on the stage in a detailed squalor of realism which to my mind distracts attention from what is interesting about them.

I wrote *Play with a Tiger* with an apparently conventional opening designed to make the audience expect a naturalistic play so that when the walls vanished towards the end of Act One they would be surprised (and I hope pleasantly shocked) to find they were not going to see this kind of play at all.

But there had to be a bridge between the opening of the play, and the long section where Anna and Dave are alone on the stage, and this bridge is one of style. This is why Anna's room is tall, bare, formal; why it has practically no furniture, save for the bed and the small clutter around it; and why there are no soft chairs or settees where the actors might lounge or sprawl. This stark set forces a certain formality of movement, stance and confrontation so that even when Dave and Anna are not alone on the stage creating their private world, there is a simplicity of style which links the two moods of the play together.

It is my intention that when the curtain comes down at the end, the audience will think: Of course! In this play no one lit cigarettes, drank tea or coffee, read newspapers, squirted soda into Scotch, or indulged in little bits of 'business' which indicated 'character'. They will realize, I hope, that they have been seeing a play which relies upon its style and its language for its effect.

DORIS LESSING

# CHARACTERS

**ANNA FREEMAN**: A woman of thirty-five, or so, who earns her living on the artistic fringes.

**DAVE MILLER**: An American, about thirty-three, who is rootless on principle.

**MARY JACKSON**: About ten years older than Anna: a widow with a grown-up son.

**TOM LATTIMER**: Who is on the point of taking a job as business manager of a woman's magazine. About thirty-five, a middle-class Englishman.

**HARRY PAINE**: Fifty-ish. A journalist.

**JANET STEVENS**: In her early twenties, the daughter of an insurance agent — American.

# Act One

The action of this play takes place in ANNA FREEMAN'S *room on the first floor of* MARY JACKSON'S *house, on a street in London with heavy traffic.* ANNA *has lived here for some years. There is another room, behind this one, used by her son, now at school; but* ANNA *sleeps and lives in this room. It is very large and looks formal because it is underfurnished. There are double doors at left-back. When they are open the landing can be seen, and part of the stairway leading up. The house was originally built for rich people and still shows signs of it. The landing and stairs are spacious and carpeted in dark red; the banisters are elegant and painted white. The upper part of the doors are of glass, and therefore the doorway has a dark red curtain, usually drawn back. The room is painted white, walls and ceilings. There is a low wide divan, covered in rough black material, in the right back corner; a window, with dark red curtains, in the right wall; a large, round, ornate mirror, on the left wall; a low shelf of books under the window. The floor is painted black and has in the centre of it a round crimson carpet. There are two stiff-looking chairs on either side of the mirror, of dark wood, and seated in dark red. The life of the room is concentrated around the divan. A low table by its head has a telephone, and is loaded with books and papers, and a small reading light. At the foot of the divan is another low table, with a typewriter, at which* ANNA *works by kneeling, or squatting, on the divan. This table has another reading light, and a record player. Around the divan is a surf of books, magazines, newspapers, records, cushions. There is a built-in cupboard, hardly noticeable until opened, in the right wall. Two paraffin heaters, of the cheap black cylindrical kind, are both lit. It is winter. The year is* 1958. *At the opening of the play the time is about nine in the evening, at its close it is four in the morning.*

[ANNA *is standing at the window, which is open at the top, her back to the room. She is wearing slacks and a sweater: these are pretty, even fashionable; the reason for the trousers is that it is hard to play Act II in a skirt.*]

[TOM *is standing behind* ANNA, *waiting, extremely exasperated. This scene between them has been going on for some time. They are both tense, irritated, miserable.*]

[TOM'S *sarcasm and pomposity are his way of protecting himself from his hurt at how he has been treated.*]

[ANNA'S *apparent casualness is how she wards off a hysteria that is only just under control. She is guilty about* TOM, *unhappy about* DAVE — *and this tension in her underlies everything she says or does until that moment towards the end of Act One when* DAVE, *because of his moral ascendancy over her, forces her to relax and smile.*]

[*A moment's silence. Then a scream and a roar of traffic, which sounds as if it is almost in the room.* TOM *loses patience, goes past* ANNA *to window, slams it shut, loudly.*]

TOM: Now say: 'I could repeat every word you've said.'

ANNA [*in quotes*]: I've scarcely seen you during the last two weeks. You always have some excuse. Mary answers the telephone and says you are out. I was under the impression we were going to be married. If I'm wrong please correct me. I simply cannot account for the change in your attitude . . . how's that?

[TOM *looks at her, gives her a small sardonic bow, goes past her to a chair which is set so he is facing half away from her. He sits in it in a pose which he has clearly been occupying previously — for* ANNA *looks at him, equally sardonic. Since the chair is hard and upright, not designed for comfort, he is almost lying in a straight line from his crossed ankles to his chin, which is upturned because he is looking with weary patience at the ceiling. His fingertips are held lightly together.*]

[ANNA, *having registered the fact that his pose is designed to annoy, goes back to the window and stands looking down.*]

ANNA: That man is still down there. Do you know, he comes every night and just stands there, hour after hour after hour. And it's so cold.

TOM: Yes, it is ... Anna, I was under the impression that my attraction for you, such as it is, of course, was that I'm rather more reliable, more responsible? than the usual run of your friends?

ANNA: Do you realize that man hasn't so much as moved a muscle since he arrived at six? There he stands, gazing up at that window. And the top half of that house is a brothel. He must have seen one of the girls in the street and fallen in love. Imagine it, I've been living here all these years and I never knew that house was a brothel. There are four Lesbians living together, and that poor sap's in love with one of them. Well, isn't it frightening?

TOM: When you walked into my flat that evening — if I may remind you of it — you said you were in search of a nice solid shoulder to weep on. You said you couldn't stand another minute of living like this. Well?

ANNA: I asked the policeman at the corner. Why yes, miss, he said, all fatherly and protective, they've been there for years and years. But don't you worry your pretty little head about a thing, we have our eyes on them all the time.

TOM: I suppose what all this amounts to is that your fascinating American is around again.

ANNA: I told you, no. I haven't seen Dave for weeks. Perhaps I should go down and tell that poor moonstruck idiot — look, you poor sap, all you've got to do is to go upstairs with fifty shillings in your hand and your goddess is yours?

TOM: And while you're about it, you could take him off for a nice cup of tea, listen to his troubles and tell him yours.

ANNA: Yes I could. Why not?

TOM: You're going to go on like this I suppose until the next time. Dave or some similarly fascinating character plays you up and you decide that good old Tom will do for a month or so?

ANNA: Tom, it's nine-fifteen. You're expected at the Jeffries at nine-thirty.

TOM: I did accept for you too.

ANNA: Yes you did, and you didn't even ask me first.

TOM: I see.

ANNA: No, you don't see. Tom, until two weeks ago you said you couldn't stand either of the Jeffries, you said, quote, they were boring, phoney and stupid. But now he's going to be your boss it's different?

TOM: No, they're still boring, phoney and stupid, but he is going to be my boss.

ANNA: You said if you took Jeffries' job, you'd be in the rat-race, stuck in the rut, and bound hand and foot to the grindstone.

TOM: I finally took that job because we were going to be married — so I thought.

ANNA: But now we're not going to be married you'll turn down the job? [*as he does not reply*] I thought not. So don't use me to justify yourself.

TOM: You really do rub things in, Anna. All right then. For a number of years I've been seeing myself as a sort of a rolling stone, a fascinating free-lance, a man of infinite possibilities. It turns out that I'm just another good middle-class citizen after all — I'm comfort-loving, conventionally unconventional, I'm not even the Don Juan I thought I was. It turns out that I'm everything I dislike most. I owe this salutary discovery to you, Anna. Thank you very much.

ANNA: Oh, not at all.

TOM [*he now gets up from the chair, and faces her, attacking hard*]: Oh my God, you stupid little romantic. Yes, that's what you are, and a prig into the bargain. Very pleased with yourself because you won't soil your hands. Writing a little review here, a little article there, an odd poem or two, a reflection on the aspect of a sidelight on the back-wash of some bloody movement or other — reading tuppenny-halfpenny novels for publishers' Mr Bloody Black's new book is or is not an advance on his last. Well, Anna, is it really worth it?

ANNA: Yes it is. I'm free to live as I like. You won't be, ever again.

TOM: And worrying all the time how you're going to find the money for what your kid wants. Do you think he's going to thank you for living like this?

ANNA: That's right. Always stick the knife in, as hard as you can, into a person's weakest spot.

TOM: An art you are not exactly a stranger to? You live here, hand to mouth, never knowing what's going to happen next, surrounding yourself with bums and neurotics and failures. As far as you're concerned anyone who has succeeded at anything at all is corrupt. [She says nothing.] Nothing to say, Anna? That's not like you.

ANNA: I was thinking, not for the first time, unfortunately, how sad it is that the exquisite understanding and intimacy of the bed doesn't last into the cold light of day.

TOM: So that's all we had in common. Thank you Anna, you've now defined me.

ANNA: All right, all right, all right. I'm sorry. What else can I say — I'm sorry.

[There is a knock on the door.]

ANNA: Come in.
TOM: Oh my God, Mary.
MARY [outside the door]: Pussy, pussy, pussy.

[A knock on the door.]

ANNA: Come in.
TOM: She's getting very deaf, isn't she?
ANNA: She doesn't know it. [as the door opens] For the Lord's sake don't say ... [she imitates him] ... I was under the impression we had said come in, if I'm wrong please correct me.

TOM: Just because you've decided to give me the boot, there's no need to knock me down and start jumping on me.

[MARY comes in, backwards, shutting the door to keep the cat out.]

MARY: No pussy, you stay there. Anna doesn't really like you, although she pretends she does. [to ANNA] That cat is more like a dog, really, he comes when I call. And he waits for me outside a door. [peeping around the edge of the door] No, puss, wait. I won't be a minute. [to ANNA] I don't know why I bothered to christen that cat Methuselah, it never gets called anything but puss. [*sprightly with an exaggerated sigh*] Really, I'm getting quite an old maid, fussing over a cat . . . If you can call a widow with a grown up son an old maid, but who'd have believed I'd have come to fussing over a cat. [*seeing* TOM] Oh, I didn't know you were here.

TOM: Didn't you see me? I said hullo.

MARY: Sometimes I think I'm getting a bit deaf. Well, what a surprise. You're quite a stranger, aren't you?

TOM: Hardly a stranger, I should have said.

MARY: Dropped in for old times' sake [TOM *is annoyed*. MARY *says to* ANNA] I thought we might go out to the pub. I'm sick of sitting and brooding. [*as* ANNA *does not respond – quick and defensive*] Oh I see, you and Tom are going out, two's company and three's none.

ANNA: Tom's going to the Jeffries.

MARY [*derisive*]: Not the Jeffries – you must be hard up for somewhere to go.

ANNA: And I think I'll stay and work.

TOM: Anna is too good for the Jeffries.

MARY: Who isn't?

[ANNA *has gone back to the window, is looking down into the street*.]

TOM [*angrily*]: Perhaps you'd like to come with me, since Anna won't.

MARY [*half aggressive, half coy*]: You and me going out together – that'd be a change. Oh, I see, you're joking. [*genuinely*] Besides, they really are so awful.

TOM: Better than going to the pub with Methuselah, perhaps?

MARY: [*with spirit*]: No, I prefer Methuselah. You don't want to bore yourself at the Jeffries. Stay and have some coffee with us.

ANNA [*her back still turned*]: It's the Royal Command.

MARY: Oh. You mean you've taken that job after all? I told Anna you would, months ago. There, Anna, I told you he would. Anna said when it actually came to the point, you'd never bring yourself to do it.

TOM. I like the idea of you and Anna laying bets as to whether the forces of good or evil would claim my soul.

MARY: Well, I mean, that's what it amounts to, doesn't it? But I always said Anna was wrong about you. Didn't I, Anna? Anna always does this. [*awkwardly*] I mean, it's not the first time, I mean to say. And I've always been right. Ah, well, as Anna says, don't you, Anna, if a man marries, he marries a woman, but if a woman marries, she marries a way of life.

TOM: Strange, but as it happens I too have been the lucky recipient of that little aphorism.

MARY: Well, you were bound to be, weren't you? [*she sees* TOM *is furious and stops*] Harry telephoned you, Anna.

ANNA: What for?

MARY: Well, I suppose now you're free he thinks he'll have another try.

TOM: May I ask — how did he know Anna was free? After all, I didn't.

MARY: Oh, don't be silly. I mean, you and Anna might not have known, but it was quite obvious to everyone else . . . well, I met Harry in the street some days ago, and he said . . .

TOM: I see.

MARY: Well, there's no need to be so stuffy about it Tom —

[*A bell rings downstairs.*]

MARY: Was that the bell? Are you expecting someone, Anna?

TOM: Of course she's expecting someone.

ANNA: No.

MARY [*who hasn't heard*]: Who are you expecting?

ANNA: Nobody.

MARY: Well, I'll go for you, I have to go down anyway. Are you in or out, Anna?

ANNA: I'm out.

MARY: It's often difficult to say, whether you are in or out, because after all, one never knows who it might be.

ANNA [*patiently*]: Mary, I really don't mind answering my bell you know.

MARY [*hastily going to the door*]: Sometimes I'm running up and down the stairs half the day, answering Anna's bell. [*as she goes out and shuts the door*] Pussy, pussy, where are you puss, puss, puss.

TOM: She's deteriorating fast, isn't she? [ANNA *patiently says nothing*] That's what you're going to be like in ten years' time if you're not careful.

ANNA: I'd rather be like Mary in ten years' time than what you're going to be like when you're all settled down and respectable.

TOM: A self-pitying old bore.

ANNA: She is also a kind warm-hearted woman with endless time for people in trouble . . . Tom, you're late, the boss waits, and you can't afford to offend him.

TOM: I remember Mary, and not so long ago either – she was quite a dish, wasn't she? If I were you I'd be scared stiff.

ANNA: Sometimes I am scared stiff. [*seriously*] Tom, her son's getting married next week.

TOM: Oh, so that's it.

ANNA: No, that's not it. She's very pleased he's getting married. And she's given them half the money she's saved – not that there's much of it. You surely must see it's going to make quite a difference to her, her son getting married?

TOM: Well he was bound to get married some time.

ANNA: Yes he was bound to get married, time marches on, every dog must have its day, one generation makes way for another, today's kittens are tomorrow's cats, life's like that.

TOM: I don't know why it is, most people think I'm quite a harmless sort of man. After ten minutes with you I feel I ought to crawl into the nearest worm-hole and die.

ANNA: We're just conforming to the well-known rule that when an affair ends, the amount of violence and unpleasantness is in direct ratio to its heat.

[*Loud laughter and voices outside* – HARRY *and* MARY.]

TOM: I thought you said you were out. Mary really is quite impossible.

ANNA: It's Harry who's impossible. He always takes it for granted one doesn't mean him.

TOM [*angry*]: And perhaps one doesn't.

ANNA: Perhaps one doesn't

TOM: Anna! Do let's try and be a bit more . . .

ANNA: Civilized? Is that the word you're looking for?

[HARRY *and* MARY *come in.*]

HARRY [*as he kisses* ANNA]: Civilized, she says. There's our Anna. I knew I'd come in and she'd be saying civilized. [*coolly, to* TOM] Oh, hullo.

TOM [*coolly*]: Well, Harry.

MARY [*who has been flirted by* HARRY *into an over-responsive state*]: Oh, Harry, you are funny sometimes. [*she laughs*] It's not what you say, when you come to think of it, it's the way you say it.

HARRY: Surely, it's what I say as well?

ANNA: Harry, I'm not in. I told Mary, I don't want to see anybody.

HARRY: Don't be silly, darling, of course you do. You don't want to see anybody, but you want to see me.

TOM [*huffy*]: Anna and I were talking.

HARRY: Of course you are, you clots. And it's high time you stopped. Look at you both. And now we should all have a drink.

TOM: Oh damn. You and Mary go and have a drink.

HARRY: That's not the way at all. Anna will come to the pub with me and weep on my shoulder, and Tom will stay and weep on Mary's.

TOM [*rallying into his smooth sarcasm*]: Harry, I yield to no one in my admiration of your tact but I really must say . . .

HARRY: Don't be silly. I got a clear picture from Mary here, of you and Anna, snarling and snapping on the verge of tears – it doesn't do at all. When a thing's finished it's finished. I know, for my sins I'm an expert.

TOM: Forgive me if I make an over-obvious point, but this really isn't one of the delightful little affairs you specialize in.

HARRY: Of course it was. You two really aren't in a position to judge. Now if you weren't Tom and Anna, you'd take one look at yourselves and laugh your heads off at the idea of your getting married.

ANNA [*she goes to the window and looks down*]: Harry, come and see me next week and I'll probably laugh my head off.

HARRY: Next week's no good at all. You won't need me then, you'll have recovered.

TOM [*immensely sarcastic*]: Surely, Harry, if Anna asks you to leave her flat, the least you can do is to . . . [ANNA *suddenly giggles.*]

HARRY: There, you see? How could you possibly marry such a pompous idiot, Anna. [*to* TOM, *affectionately*] Anna can't possibly marry such an idiot, Tom. Anna doesn't like well-ordered citizens, like you, anyway.

MARY: I don't know how you can say well-ordered. He was just another lame duck until now.

HARRY: But he's not a lame duck any more. He's going to work for Jeffries, and he'll be administering to the spiritual needs of the women of the nation through the 'Ladies Own.'

TOM: I'm only going to be on the business side. I won't be responsible for the rubbish they — [*He stops, annoyed with himself.* HARRY *and* MARY *laugh at him.*]

HARRY: There you are, he's a solid respectable citizen already.

TOM [*to* HARRY]: It's not any worse than the rag you work for is it?

HARRY [*reacts to* TOM *with a grimace that says touché! and turns to* ANNA]: When are you going to get some comfortable furniture into this room?

ANNA [*irritated almost to tears*]: Oh sit on the floor, go away, stop nagging.

HARRY: Don't be so touchy. The point I'm trying to make is, Tom'd never put up with a woman like you, he's going to have a house with every modern convenience and everything just so . . . Anna, what've you done with Dave?

ANNA: I haven't seen him for weeks.

HARRY: That's silly, isn't it now?

ANNA: No.

HARRY: Now I'm going to give you a lot of good advice, Anna and . . .

TOM: Fascinating, isn't it? Harry giving people advice.

MARY: Harry may not know how to get his own life into order,
but actually he's rather good at other people's.
HARRY: What do you mean, my life is in perfect order.
TOM: Indeed? May I ask how your wife is?
HARRY [in a much used formula]: Helen is wonderful, delightful,
she is very happy and she loves me dearly.
TOM [with a sneer]: How nice.
HARRY: Yes, it is. And that's what I'm going to explain to you,
Anna. Look at Helen. She's like you, she likes interesting
weak men like me, and . . .
TOM: Weak is not the word I'd have chosen, I must say.
MARY: Surely not weak, Harry?
ANNA: Weak is new, Harry. Since when, weak?
HARRY: I'll explain. It came to me in a flash, one night when
I was driving home very late – it was dawn, to be precise,
you see, weak men like me . . .
ANNA [suddenly serious]: Harry, I'm not in the mood.
HARRY: Of course you are. We are always in the mood to talk
about ourselves. I'm talking about you, Anna. You're like
Helen. Now what does Helen say? She says, she doesn't mind
who I have affairs with provided they are women she'd like
herself.
TOM: Charming.
MARY: But Harry, Helen's got to say something . . . well, I
mean to say.
ANNA: I simply can't stand your damned alibis.
HARRY: Tom must have been bad for you, Anna, if you're
going to get all pompous. Helen and I . . .
ANNA [snapping]: Harry, you forget I know Helen very
well.
HARRY [not realizing her mood]: Of course you do. And so do
I. And you ought to take on Dave the way Helen's taken
me on . . .
ANNA: Harry, go away.
HARRY [still blithe]: No, Anna. I've been thinking. You've got
to marry Dave. He needs you.
[MARY makes a warning gesture at HARRY, indicating ANNA.]
[to MARY] Don't be silly, darling. [to ANNA again] Helen knows

I'll always come back to her. Anna, Dave needs you. Have
a heart. What'll Dave do?

ANNA [*snapping into hysterical resentment*]: I'll tell you what he'll
do. He'll do what you did. You married Helen who
was very much in love with you. When she had turned
into just another boring housewife and mother you
began philandering. She had no alternative but to stay
put.

HARRY: Anna, Anna, Anna!

ANNA: Oh shut up. I know Helen, I know exactly what sort
of hell she's had with you.

HARRY: Tom, you really have been bad for Anna, you've made
her all bitchy.

ANNA: Dave will marry some girl who's in love with him. Oh,
he'll fight every inch of the way, of course. Then there'll be
children and he'll be free to do as he likes. He'll have a
succession of girls, and in between each one he'll go back
and weep on his wife's shoulder because of his unfortunately
weak character. Weak like hell. She'll forgive him all right.
He'll even use her compliance as an additional attraction for
the little girls, just as you do. My wife understands me, he'll
say, with a sloppy look on his face. She knows what I'm
like. She'll always be there to take me back. God almighty,
what a man.

HARRY: Anna, you little bitch.

ANNA: That's right. But there's just one thing, Dave shouldn't
have picked on me. I'm economically independent. I have
no urge for security so I don't have to sell myself out. And
I have a child already, so there's no way of making me
helpless, is there, dear weak, helpless Harry?

HARRY: Mary, you should have told me Anna was in such a
bitchy mood and I wouldn't have come up.

MARY: But I did tell you, and you said, 'Well Anna won't be
bitchy with me.'

[*The door bell, downstairs.*]

MARY: I'll go.

ANNA: Mary, I'm out.

MARY: Well don't blame me for Harry, he insisted. [*as she goes out*] Pussy, pussy, puss, puss.

HARRY: I can't think what Mary would do if Anna did get married.

TOM [*spitefully*]: They are rather like an old married couple, aren't they?

[ANNA *pulls down the window with a crash and turns her back on them.*]

HARRY: But so nice to drop in on for aid and comfort when in trouble. [*to* ANNA'S *back*] Anna, I'm in trouble.

ANNA: Don't worry, you'll be in love with someone else in a few weeks.

HARRY [*humorous but serious*]: But I won't. This girl, my poppet, she's getting married. [*as* ANNA *shrugs*] For God's sake woman, shut the window, it's freezing. [ANNA *shuts it, but remains looking down.*] She met some swine at a party — actually he's very nice. A handsome young swine — he really is nice. She's marrying him — actually, I advised her to. Anna!

ANNA: Did you expect her to hang round for the rest of her life in a state of single blessedness because you didn't want to break up your happy home with Helen? [*she turns, sees his face, which is genuinely miserable*] Oh all right. I'm sorry. I'm very sorry. [*She puts her arms around him.*]

HARRY: There's my Anna. [*to* TOM] I'm sure you've never seen this side of her, but she is a sweet girl, at heart.

TOM: Well, now you've gained your little need of sympathy from Anna, perhaps I may be permitted to say a word or two?

HARRY: No. You two should just kiss and say goodbye and stop tormenting each other.

TOM: Anna I know that what goes on in the street is a hundred times more interesting than I am, but . . .

HARRY: Of course it is, she's waiting for Dave.

ANNA: I'm not waiting for Dave.

[*She comes away from the window. Sits on the bed, her head in her hands.*]

TOM: I want to talk to Anna.

MARY [*from downstairs*]: Puss, puss, puss, puss.

TOM [*mocking her*]: Puss, puss, puss, puss.

HARRY: Mary should get married. Anna, you should make Mary get married before it's too late.

TOM: Before it's too late!

ANNA: Mary could marry if she wanted.

TOM [*derisively*]: Then why doesn't she?

ANNA: Strange as it might seem to you, she doesn't want to get married just for the sake of getting married.

HARRY: Yes, but that's all very well, Anna. It's all right for you – you're such a self-contained little thing. But not for Mary. You should get her married regardless to the first clot who comes along.

ANNA: I – self-contained!

TOM: Yes, it's true – self-contained!

MARY [*from downstairs*]: Pussy, pussy, yes come here, puss, puss, puss, puss.

TOM [*to* HARRY]: She's getting worse. [*as* ANNA *stiffens up*] Yes, all right, Anna, but it's true. [*to* HARRY] She's man-crazy . . .

HARRY: Oh you silly ass.

TOM: Well she is. She's crazy for a man, wide open, if you so much as smile at her, she responds. And Anna says she doesn't want to marry. Who are you fooling, Anna?

ANNA [*sweetly*]: Perhaps she prefers to be sex-starved than to marry an idiot. Which is more than can be said about most men.

HARRY: Now Anna, don't start, Anna, Tom's a nice man, but he's pompous. [*to* TOM] You're a pompous ass, admit it, Tom.

TOM: All I said was, Mary's man-crazy.

ANNA [*on the warpath*]: Do you know how Tom was living before he started with me?

HARRY: Yes, of course. Anna, don't make speeches at us!

TOM: Well, how was I living before I started with you?

HARRY: Oh, my God.

ANNA: What is known as a bachelor's life – Tom's own nice inimitable version of it. He sat in his nice little flat, and round

about ten at night, if he felt woman-crazy enough, he rang
up one of three girls, all of whom were in love with him.

HARRY: Christ knows why.

ANNA: Imagine it, the telephone call at bedtime — are you free
tonight, Elspeth, Penelope, Jessica? One of them came over,
a drink or a cup of coffee, a couple of hours of bed, and
then a radio-taxi home.

HARRY: Anna!

ANNA: Oh from time to time he explained to them that they
mustn't think his kind attentions to them meant anything.

HARRY: Anna, you're a bore when you get like this.

TOM: Yes, you are.

ANNA: Then don't call Mary names.

[MARY *comes in.*]

MARY [*suspicious*]: You were talking about me?

ANNA: No, about me.

MARY: Oh I thought it was about me. [*to* ANNA] There's a
girl wants to see you. She says it's important. She wouldn't
give her name.

ANNA [*she is thinking*]: I see.

MARY: But she's an American girl. It's the wrong time of the
year — summer's for Americans.

ANNA: An American girl.

MARY: One of those nice bright neat clean American girls, how
they do it, I don't know, all I know is that you can tell from
a hundred yards off they'd rather be seen dead than with
their legs or their armpits unshaved, ever so antiseptic, she
looked rather sweet really.

HARRY: Tell her to go away and we'll all wait for you. Come
on, Tom.

TOM: I'm staying.

HARRY: Come on, Mary, give me a nice cup of coffee.

MARY: It's a long time since you and I had a good gossip.

[HARRY *and* MARY *go out, arm in arm.*]

TOM: Well, who is she?

ANNA: I don't know.

TOM: I don't believe you.

ANNA: You never do.

[MARY'S *voice, and the voice of an American girl, outside on the stairs.*]

[JANET STEVENS *comes in. She is a neat attractive girl of about 22. She is desperately anxious and trying to hide it.*]

JANET: Are you Anna Freeman?

ANNA: Yes. And this is Tom Lattimer.

JANET: I am Janet Stevens. [*she has expected* ANNA *to know the name*] Janet Stevens.

ANNA: How do you do?

JANET: Janet Stevens from Philadelphia. [*as* ANNA *still does not react*] I hope you will excuse me for calling on you like this.

ANNA: Not at all.

[JANET *looks at* TOM. ANNA *looks at* TOM. TOM *goes to the window, turns his back.*]

JANET [*still disbelieving* ANNA]: I thought you would know my name.

ANNA: No.

TOM: But she has been expecting you all afternoon.

JANET [*at sea*]: All afternoon?

ANNA [*angry*]: No, it's not true.

JANET: I don't understand, you were expecting me this afternoon?

ANNA: No. But may I ask, how you know me?

JANET: Well, we have a friend in common. Dave Miller.

TOM [*turning, furious*]: You could have said so, couldn't you, Anna?

ANNA: But I didn't know.

TOM: You didn't know. Well I'm going. You've behaved disgracefully.

ANNA: Very likely. However just regard me as an unfortunate lapse from the straight and narrow on your journey to respectability.

[TOM *goes out, slamming the door.*]

ANNA [politely] That was my    fiancé.
JANET: Oh, Dave didn't say you were engaged.
ANNA: He didn't know. And besides, I'm not 'engaged' any longer.

[A silence. ANNA looks with enquiry at JANET, who tries to speak and fails.]

ANNA: Please sit down, Miss Stevens.

[JANET looks around for somewhere to sit, sits on a chair, smiles socially. Being a well brought up young lady, and in a situation she does not understand, she is using her good manners as a last-ditch defence against breaking down.]

[ANNA looks at her, waiting.]

JANET: It's this way, you see Dave and I . . . [At ANNA's ironical look she stops.] . . . What a pretty room, I do so love these old English houses, they have such . . .

[ANNA looks at her: do get a move on.]

JANET: My father gave me a vacation in Europe for passing my college examinations. Yes, even when I was a little girl he used to promise me — if you do well at college I'll give you a vacation in Europe. Well, I've seen France and Italy now, but I really feel most at home in England than any-where. I do love England. Of course our family was English, way back of course, and I feel that roots are important, don't you?
ANNA: Miss Stevens, what did you come to see me for?
JANET: Dave always says he thinks women should have careers. I suppose that's why he admires you so much. Though of course, you do wear well. But I say to him, Dave, if you work at marriage then it is a career . . . sometimes he makes fun because I took domestic science and home care and child care as my subjects in college, but I say to him, Dave marriage is important, Dave, I believe that marriage and the family are the most rewarding career a woman can have, that's why I took home care as my first subject because I believe a healthy

and well-adjusted marriage is the basis for a healthy nation.

ANNA: You're making me feel deficient in patriotism.

JANET: Oh, Dave said that too . . . [*she almost breaks down, pulls herself together: fiercely*] You're patronizing me. I don't think you should patronize me.

ANNA: Miss Stevens, do let's stop this. Listen to me. I haven't seen Dave for weeks. Is that what you came here to find out?

JANET: I know that you are such old friends. He talks about you a great deal.

ANNA: I've no doubt he does. [*She waits for* JANET *to go on, then goes on herself.*] There's a hoary psychological joke – if I can use the word joke for a situation like this – about the way the betrayed women of the heartless libertine get together to lick their wounds – have you come here to make common cause with me over Dave? Because forgive me for saying so, but I don't think you and I have anything in common but the fact we've both slept with Dave. And that is not enough for the basis of a beautiful friendship.

JANET: No! It wasn't that at all, I came because . . . [*she stops*]

ANNA: I see. Then you've come because you're pregnant. Well, how far have you got?

JANET: Five months.

ANNA: I see. And you haven't told him.

ANNA: I knew if I told him he'd give me money and . . . well I love him. It would be good for him to have some responsibility wouldn't it?

ANNA: I see.

JANET: Yes, I know how it looks, trapping a man. But when I was pregnant I was so happy, and only afterwards I thought – yes, I know how it looks, trapping a man, but he said he loved me, he said he loved me.

ANNA: But why come and tell me? [*as* JANET *doesn't answer*] He's ditched you, is that it?

JANET: No! Of course he hasn't. [*cracking*] I haven't seen him in days. I haven't seen him. Where is he, you've got to tell me where he is. I've got to tell him about the baby.

ANNA: But I don't know where he is.

JANET: You have to tell me. When he knows about the baby he'll ... [as ANNA *shrugs*] Ah come on now, who do you think you're kidding? Well I've got his baby, you haven't. You can't do anything about that, can you. I've got his baby, I've got him.

ANNA: Very likely.

JANET: But what can I do? I want to be married. I'm just an ordinary girl and I want to be married, what's wrong with that?

ANNA: There's nothing wrong with that. But I haven't seen Dave, and I don't know where he is, and so there's nothing I can do. [*finally*] And you shouldn't have come to me.

[JANET *goes out.*]

ANNA [*almost in tears*]: Oh Christ. [*stopping the tears, angrily*] Damn. Damn.

[*She goes to window. At once* MARY *comes in.*]

MARY: Well who was she? [ANNA *turns her back to hide her face from* MARY.] Was she one of Dave's girls? [ANNA *nods.* MARY *moves so that she can see* ANNA'S *face.*] Well, you knew there was one, didn't you? [ANNA *nods.*] Well, then? [ANNA *nods.*]

ANNA: All right, Mary.

[MARY *is in a jubilant mood. She has been flirting with* HARRY. *Now, seeing* ANNA *is apparently all right, she says what she came in to say.*]

MARY: Harry and I are going out. There's a place he knows we can get drinks. I told him you wouldn't be interested. [*The telephone starts ringing.*] Aren't you going to answer it? [*as* ANNA *shakes her head*] Odd, we've known each other all these years. He's really sweet, Harry. You can say what you like, but it's nice to have a man to talk to for a change — after all, how many men are there you can really talk to? [*The telephone stops.*] Anna, what are you in this state for?

ANNA: What I can't stand is, the way he makes use of me. Do you know Mary, all this time he's been letting her know I'm in the background?

MARY: Well you are, aren't you?

ANNA: 'But Janet, you must understand this doesn't mean anything, because the woman I really love is Anna.' He's not even married to me, but he uses me as Harry uses Helen.

MARY: [*not wanting to hear anything against* HARRY *at this moment*] Oh I don't know. After all, perhaps Helen doesn't mind. They've been married so long.

ANNA: It really is remarkable how all Dave's young ladies turn up here sooner or later. He talks about me – oh, quite casually, of course, until they go round the bend with frustration and curiosity, and they just have to come up to see what the enemy looks like. Well I can't be such a bitch as all that, because I didn't say, 'My dear Miss Stevens, you're the fifth to pay me a social call in three years.'

MARY: But you have been engaged to Tom.

ANNA: Yes. All right.

MARY: It's funny, me and Harry knowing each other for so long and then suddenly . . .

ANNA: Mary! The mood Harry's in somebody's going to get hurt.

MARY: It's better to get hurt than to live shut up.

ANNA: After losing that little poppet of his to matrimony he'll be looking for solace.

MARY [*offended*]: Why don't you concern yourself with Tom? Or with Dave? Harry's not your affair. I'm just going out with him. [*as she goes out*] Nice to have a night out for a change, say what you like.

[*The telephone rings.* ANNA *snatches off the receiver, wraps it in a blanket, throws it on the bed.*

ANNA: I'm not talking to you, Dave Miller, you can rot first.

[*She goes to the record player, puts on Mahalia Jackson's 'I'm on My Way', goes to the mirror, looks into it. This is a long antagonistic look.*]

ANNA [*to her reflection*]: All right then, I do wear well.

[*She goes deliberately to a drawer, takes out a large piece of black cloth, unfolds it, drapes it over the mirror.*]

ANNA [to the black cloth]: And a fat lot of good that does me.

[She now switches out the light. The room is tall, shadowy, with two patterns of light from the paraffin heaters reflected on the ceiling. She goes to the window, flings it up.]

ANNA [to the man on the pavement]: You poor fool, why don't you go upstairs, the worst that can happen is that the door will be shut in your face.

[A knock on the door – a confident knock.]

ANNA: If you come in here, Dave Miller . . .

[DAVE comes in. He is crew cut, wears a sloppy sweater and jeans. Carries a small duffle bag. ANNA turns her back and looks out of the window. DAVE stops the record player. He puts the telephone receiver back on the rest. Turns on the light.]

DAVE: Why didn't you answer the telephone?
ANNA: Because I have nothing to say.
DAVE [in a parody of an English upper-middle-class voice]: I see no point at all in discussing it.
ANNA [in the same voice]: I see no point at all in discussing it.

[DAVE stands beside ANNA at the window.]

DAVE [in the easy voice of their intimacy]: I've been in the telephone box around the corner ringing you.
ANNA: Did you see my visitor?
DAVE: No.
ANNA: What a pity.
DAVE: I've been standing in the telephone box ringing you and watching that poor bastard on the pavement.
ANNA: He's there every night. He comes on his great black dangerous motor bike. He wears a black leather jacket and big black boots. He looks like an outrider for death in a Cocteau film – and he has the face of a frightened little boy.
DAVE: It's lurve, it's lurve, it's lurve.
ANNA: It's love.

[Now they stare at each other, antagonists, and neither gives way.

[DAVE *suddenly grins and does a mocking little dance step. He stands grinning at her.* ANNA *hits him as hard as she can. He staggers. He goes to the other side of the carpet, where he sits cross-legged, his face in his hands.*]

DAVE: Jesus, Anna.

ANNA [*mocking*]: Oh, quite so.

DAVE: You still love me, that's something.

ANNA: It's lurve, it's lurve, it's lurve.

DAVE: Yes. I had a friend once. He cheated on his wife, he came in and she laid his cheek open with the flat-iron.

ANNA [*quoting him*]: 'That I can understand' — a great country, America.

DAVE [*in appeal*]: Anna.

ANNA: No.

DAVE: I've been so lonely for you.

ANNA: Where have you been the last week?

DAVE [*suspicious*]: Why the last *week*?

ANNA: I'm interested.

DAVE: Why the last week? [*a pause*] Ringing you and getting no reply.

ANNA: Why ringing *me*?

DAVE: Who else? Anna, I will not be treated like this.

ANNA: Then, go away.

DAVE: We've been through this before. Can't we get it over quickly?

ANNA: No.

DAVE: Come and sit down. And turn out the lights.

ANNA: No.

DAVE: I didn't know it was as bad as that this time.

ANNA: How long did you think you could go on — you think you can make havoc as you like, and nothing to pay for it, ever?

DAVE: Pay? What for? You've got it all wrong, as usual.

ANNA: I'm not discussing it then.

DAVE: 'I'm not discussing it.' Well, I'm saying nothing to you while you've got your bloody middle-class English act on, it drives me mad.

ANNA: Middle class English. I'm Australian.

DAVE: You've assimilated so well.

ANNA [*in an Australian accent*]: I'll say it like this then — I'll say it any way you like — I'm not discussing it. I'm discussing nothing with you when you're in your role of tuppence a dozen street corner Romeo. [*in English*] It's the same in any accent.

DAVE [*getting up and doing his blithe dance step*]: It's the same in any accent. [*sitting down again*] Baby, you've got it wrong. [ANNA *laughs.*] I tell you, you've got it wrong, baby.

ANNA [*in American*]: But baby, it doesn't mean anything, let's have a little fun together, baby, just you and me — just a little fun, baby . . . [*in Australian*] Ah, damn your guts, you stupid, irresponsible little . . . [*in English*] Baby, baby, baby — the anonymous baby. Every woman is baby, for fear you'd whisper the wrong name into the wrong ear in the dark.

DAVE: In the dark with you I use your name, Anna.

ANNA: You *used* my name.

DAVE: Ah, hell, man, well. Anna beat me up and be done with it and get it over. [*a pause*] OK, I know it. I don't know what gets into me; OK I'm still a twelve-year-old slum kid standing on a street corner in Chicago, watching the expensive broads go by and wishing I had the dough to buy them all. OK, I know it. You know it. [*a pause*] OK and I'm an American God help me, and it's no secret to the world that there's bad man–woman trouble in America. [*a pause*] And everywhere else, if it comes to that. OK, I do my best. But how any man can be faithful to one woman beats me. OK, so one day I'll grow up. Maybe.

ANNA: Maybe.

DAVE [*switching to black aggression*]: God, how I hate your smug female guts. All of you — there's never anything free — everything to be paid for. Every time, an account rendered. Every time, when you're swinging free there's a moment when the check lies on the table — pay up, pay up, baby.

ANNA: Have you come here to get on to one of your anti-woman kicks?

DAVE: Well I'm not being any woman's pet, and that's what

you all want. [*leaping up and doing his mocking dance step*] I've kept out of all the traps so far, and I'm going to keep out.

ANNA: So you've kept out of all the traps.

DAVE: That's right. And I'm not going to stand for you either – mother of the world, the great womb, the eternal conscience. I like women, but I'm going to like them my way and not according to the rules laid down by the incorporated mothers of the universe.

ANNA: Stop it, stop it, stop boasting.

DAVE: But Anna, you're as bad. There's always a moment when you become a sort of flaming sword of retribution.

ANNA: At which moment – have you asked yourself? You and I are so close we know everything about each other – and then suddenly, out of the clear blue sky, you start telling me lies like – lies out of a corner-boy's jest book. I can't stand it.

DAVE [*shouting at her*]: Lies – I never tell you lies.

ANNA: Oh hell, Dave.

DAVE: Well you're not going to be my conscience. I will not let you be my conscience.

ANNA: Amen and hear hear. But why do you make me your conscience?

DAVE [*deflating*]: I don't know. [*with grim humour*] I'm an American. I'm in thrall to the great mother.

ANNA: Well I'm not an American.

DAVE [*shouting*]: No, but you're a woman, and at bottom you're the same as the whole lousy lot of . . .

ANNA: Get out of here then. Get out.

DAVE [*he sits cross-legged, on the edge of the carpet, his head in his hands*]: Jesus.

ANNA: You're feeling guilty so you beat me up. I won't let you.

DAVE: Come here.

[ANNA *goes to him, kneels opposite him, lays her two hands on his diaphragm.*]

Yes, like that. [*he suddenly relaxes, head back, eyes closed*] Anna, when I'm away from you I'm cut off from something

— I don't know what it is. When you put your hands on
me, I begin to breathe.

ANNA: Oh. [*She lets her hands drop and stands up.*]

DAVE: Where are you going?

[ANNA *goes back to the window. A silence. A wolf-whistle from
the street. Another.*]

ANNA: He's broken his silence. He's calling her. Deep calls to
deep.

[*Another whistle.* ANNA *winces.*]

DAVE: You've missed me?

ANNA: All the time.

DAVE: What have you been doing?

ANNA: Working a little.

DAVE: What else?

ANNA: I said I'd marry Tom, then I said I wouldn't.

DAVE [*dismissing it*]: I should think not.

ANNA [*furious*]: O-h-h-h.

DAVE: Seriously, what?

ANNA: I've been coping with Mary – her son's marrying.

DAVE [*heartily*]: Good for him. Well, it's about time.

ANNA: Oh quite so.

DAVE [*mimicking her*]: Oh quite so.

ANNA [*dead angry*]: I've also spent hours of every day with
Helen, Harry's ever-loving wife.

DAVE: Harry's my favourite person in London.

ANNA: And you are his. Strange, isn't it?

DAVE: We understand each other.

ANNA: And Helen and I understand each other.

DAVE [*hastily*]: Now, Anna.

ANNA: Helen's cracking up. Do you know what Harry did?
He came to her, because he knew this girl of his was thinking
of getting married, and he said: Helen, you know I love you,
but I can't live without her. He suggested they should all
live together in the same house – he, Helen and his girl.
Regularizing things, he called it.

DAVE [*deliberately provocative*]: Yeah? Sounds very attractive to me.

ANNA: Yes, I thought it might. Helen said to him – who's going to share your bed? Harry said, well, obviously they couldn't all sleep in the same bed, but . . .

DAVE: Anna, stop it.

ANNA: Helen said it was just possible that the children might be upset by the arrangement.

DAVE: I was waiting for that – the trump card – you can't do that, it might upset the kiddies. Well not for me, I'm out.

ANNA [*laughing*]: Oh are you?

DAVE: Yes. [ANNA *laughs.*] Have you finished?

ANNA: No. Harry and Helen. Helen said she was going to leave him. Harry said: 'But darling, you're too old to get another man now and . . .'

DAVE [*mocking*]: Women always have to pay – and may it long remain that way.

ANNA: Admittedly there's one advantage to men like you and Harry. You are honest.

DAVE: Anna, listen, whenever I cheat on you it takes you about two weeks to settle into a good temper again. Couldn't we just speed it up and get it over with?

ANNA: Get it over with. [*she laughs*]

DAVE: The laugh is new. What's so funny?

[*A wolf-whistle from the street. Then a sound like a wolf howling.* ANNA *slams the window up.*]

DAVE: Open that window.

ANNA: No, I can't stand it.

DAVE: Anna, I will not have you shutting yourself up. I won't have you spitting out venom and getting all bitter and vengeful. Open that window.

[ANNA *opens it. Stands by it, passive.*]

Come and sit down. And turn the lights out.

[*As she does not move, he turns out the light. The room as before: two patterned circles of light on the ceiling from the paraffin lamps.*]

ANNA: Dave, it's no point starting all over again.

DAVE: But baby, you and I will always be together, one way or another.

ANNA: You're crazy.

DAVE: In a good cause. [*he sits cross-legged on the edge of the carpet and waits*] Come and sit. [ANNA *slowly sits, opposite him. He smiles at her. She slowly smiles back. As she smiles, the walls fade out. They are two small people in the city, the big, ugly, baleful city all around them, over-shadowing them.*]

DAVE: There baby, that's better.

ANNA: OK.

DAVE: I don't care what you do – you can crack up if you like, or you can turn Lesbian. You can take to drink. You can even get married. But I won't have you shutting yourself up.

[*A lorry roars. A long wolf-whistle. Shrill female voices from the street.*]

ANNA: Those girls opposite quarrel. I hate it. Last night they were rolling in the street and pulling each other's hair and screaming.

DAVE: OK. But you're not to shut it out. You're not to shut anything out.

ANNA: I'll try.

[*She very slowly gets to her feet, stands concentrating.*]

DAVE: That's right. Now, who are you?

**END OF ACT ONE**

# Act Two

[ANNA *and* DAVE, *in the same positions as at the end of Act One. No time has passed. The lights are out. The walls seemed to have vanished, so that the room seems part of the street. There is a silence. A lorry roars*]

DAVE: Who are you?
ANNA [*in English*]: Anna Freeman.
DAVE: OK. Go, then.

[*A silence.*]

ANNA: I can't. I'm all in pieces.
DAVE: Then go back. Who are you now?
ANNA [*she slowly stands up, at the edge of the carpet*]: Anna.
DAVE: Anna who?
ANNA [*in Australian*]: Anna MacClure from Brisbane [*in English*] The trouble is, she gets further and further away. She's someone else. I know if she goes altogether then I'm done for. [*a pause*] [*in Australian*] The smell of petrol. In a broken-down old jalopy – six of us. It's night. There's a great shining moon. We've been dancing. I'm with Jack. We've stopped at the edge of the road by a petrol pump. All the others are singing and shouting and the petrol pump attendant's angry as a cross cat. Jack says, 'Anna, let's get married.' [*Speaking to* JACK] 'No, Jack, what's all this about, getting married. I want to live, Jack. I want to travel. I want to see the world . . . Yes, I know, but I don't want kids yet. I don't want . . .' [*to* DAVE] He says, 'Anna you'll be unhappy. I feel it in my bones, you'll be unhappy.' [*she talks back to* JACK] 'I don't care, I tell you. I know if I marry you, you'll be for the rest of my life. You aren't the world Jack . . . All right, then I'll be unhappy. But I want a choice. Don't you see, I want a

choice. [*she crouches down, her hands over her face*] Let's have the lights Dave.

DAVE: Wait. Go back some more – that's not Anna MacClure the Australian. That's Anna MacClure who's already half in Europe.

ANNA: But it's so hard.

DAVE: Breathe slowly and go. Who are you?

ANNA [*slowly standing*] [*in a child's voice, Australian*]: Anna MacClure.

DAVE: Where?

ANNA: On the porch of our house. I've quarrelled with my mother. [*she stands talking to her mother*] I'm not going to be like you, ma, I'm not, I'm not. You're stuck here, you never think of anything but me and my brother and the house. You're old ma, you're stupid. [*listening while her mother lectures her*] Yah, I don't care. When I grow up I'm never going to be married, I'm not going to get old and dull. I'm going to live with my brother on an island and swim and catch fish and . . . [*she sings*] The moon is in my windowpane, the moon is in my bed, I'll race the moon across the sky and eat it for my bread. I don't care, ma, I don't care . . . [*She dances a blithe, defiant dance. In English*] Dave, Dave, did you see? That was just like you.

[DAVE *gets up and does his blithe defiant dance beside her on the carpet. He mocks her.* ANNA *furious, leaps over and smacks him.*]

ANNA: 'There, stupid child, you're wicked and stupid you're not going to defy me, so you think you'll defy me . . .'

[*They both at the same moment crouch down in their former positions on either side of the carpet.*]

ANNA: Let me have the light on now, please Dave.

[DAVE *switches it on, the room becomes the room again.* DAVE *returns to where he was.*]

DAVE [*patting the carpet beside him*]: Anna.

ANNA: No.

DAVE: Let me love you.

ANNA: No.

DAVE [*laughing and confident*]: You will, Anna, so why not now?

ANNA: You'll never love me again, never never never.

DAVE [*suddenly scared*]: Why not? Why not?

ANNA: You know why.

DAVE: I swear I don't.

ANNA: What am I going to be without you, what shall I do?

DAVE: But baby, I'm here.

ANNA: And what are you going to do with Janet?

DAVE: Janet?

ANNA: Janet Stephens, from Philadelphia.

DAVE: What about her?

ANNA: You don't know her, of course.

DAVE: She's a friend of mine, that's all.

ANNA: Do you know Dave, if I walked into your room and found you in bed with a girl and said Dave, who is that girl, you'd say what girl? I don't see any girl, it's just your sordid imagination.

DAVE: Some time you've got to learn to trust me.

ANNA: What you mean by trust is, you tell me some bloody silly lie and I just nod my head and smile.

DAVE [*inside the wild man*]: That's right baby, you should just nod your head and smile.

ANNA: You mean, it's got nothing to do with me.

DAVE: That's right, it's got nothing to do with you.

[ANNA *withdraws from him into herself.*]

DAVE: Ah hell, Anna, she means nothing to me.

ANNA: Then it's terrible.

[*A pause.*]

DAVE: I don't understand why I do the things I do. I go moseying along, paying my way and liking myself pretty well, then I'm sounding off like something, and people start looking at me in a certain way, and I think, Hey, man is that you? Is that you there, Dave Miller? He's taken over again, the wild man, the mad man. And I even stand on one side and watch pretty awed when you come to think of it. Yes, awed, that's the word. You should be awed too, Anna, instead of getting scared. I can't stand it when you're scared of me.

ANNA: I simply want to run out of the way.

DAVE: The way of what? Go on, tell, I want to know.

ANNA: I want to hide from the flick-knives, from the tomahawks.

DAVE [*with a loud, cruel laugh — he is momentarily inside the wild man*]: Jesus. Bloody Englishwoman, middle-class lady, that's what you are. [*mimicking her*], Flick-knives and tomahawks — how refined.

ANNA [*in the voice of* ANNA MACCLURE]: Dave, man, stand up and let it go, let it go.

[DAVE *slowly stands. He switches off the light — the walls vanish, the city comes up. Back on the carpet, stands relaxed.*]

ANNA: Who are you?

DAVE: Dave Miller, the boss of the gang, South Street, Al Capone's territory . . . Chicago.

ANNA: What's your name?

DAVE: Dave Miller.

ANNA: No, in your fantasy.

DAVE: Baby Face Nelson. No, but the way I dreamed him up, he was a sort of Robin Hood, stealing from the rich to give to the poor.

ANNA: Oh, don't be so childish.

DAVE: That was the point of this exercise I thought.

ANNA: Sorry. Go ahead.

DAVE: I'm fifteen years old. I'm wearing a sharp hat, such a sweet sharp hat — pork-pie, cleft in the middle, set on side. The hat is in dark green. My jacket is two yards wide across the shoulders, nipped in at the waist, and skirted. In a fine, sweet cinnamon brown. Trousers in forest green, very fancy. My shirt is the finest money can buy, one dollar fifty, at Holy Moses Cut Price Emporium. In deciduous mauve. My tie is orange and black in lightening stripes. I wear velveteen spats, buttoned sweetly up the side, in hearth-rug white. I have a key-chain with a key on it, probably about six feet long, which could sweep the pavement if it hung free, but it never does, because we stand, lounging on the street corner, our home, men of the world, twirling the chain between our fingers, hour after hour through the afternoons and evenings. That year I'm a shoe-shine boy, a news-boy and a drug-store assistant. But my life, my real sweet life is on the pavement. [*speaking to someone*] Jedd, see that broad? [*waits for an answer*] Gee, some dish, bet she's hot. [*waits again*] See that dame there, Jesus Christ. [*he wolf-whistles*]

[ANNA *swanks, bottom wagging in front of him.* DAVE *whistles after her. He is echoed by a wolf-whistle from the street.* ANNA *wheels at the window to shut it.*]

DAVE: I told you, keep it open.

[ANNA *returns, squatting on the edge of the carpet.*]

DAVE: Jesus, Anna, when I think of that kid, of all us kids, it makes me want to cry.
ANNA: Then cry.
DAVE: The year of our Lord, 1936, all our parents out of work, and World War II on top of us and we didn't know it.
ANNA: Did you carry a knife?
DAVE: We all did.
ANNA: Ever use it?
DAVE: Hell no, I told you, we were fine idealistic kids. That was my anarchist period. We stood twirling our keychains on the corner of the street, eyeing the broads and I quoted great chunks out of Kroptkin to the guys. Anyone who joined my gang had to be an anarchist. When I had my socialist period, they had to be socialists.
ANNA: Go on.
DAVE: Isn't it enough?
ANNA: I'm waiting for the tomahawk. You're seven years old and you scalp all the nasty adults who don't understand you.
DAVE: OK. I was a Red Indian nine-tenths of my childhood. OK. [*in his parody of an English upper-class accent*] There is no point whatever in discussing it . . . OK. Somewhere in my

psyche is a tomahawk-twirling Red Indian . . . Anna/ Lis
you know what's wrong with America?

ANNA: Yes.

DAVE: At the street corners now the kids are not prepared to
fight the world. They fight each other. Every one of us, we
were prepared to take on the whole world single-handed.
Not any longer, they know better, they're scared. A healthy
country has kids, every John Doe of them knowing he can
lick the whole world, single-handed. Not any more.

ANNA: I know.

DAVE: You know. But you're scared to talk. Everyone knows
but they're scared to talk. There's a great dream dead in
America. You look at us and see prosperity – and loneliness.
Prosperity and men and women in trouble with each other.
Prosperity and people wondering what life is for. Prosperity
– and conformity. You look at us and you know it's your
turn now. We've pioneered the golden road for you . . .

ANNA: Who are you lecturing, Anna MacClure?

DAVE: OK, OK, OK. [he flops face down on the carpet]

[ANNA puts her arms around his shoulders.]

DAVE: If you think I'm any safer to touch when I'm flat than
when I'm mobile you're wrong. [He tries to pull her down.
She pulls away.] OK. [pause] Did I tell you I went to a
psycho-analyst? Yeah, I'm a good American after all, I went
to a psycho-analyst.

ANNA [mocking him]: Do tell me about your psycho-analysis.

DAVE: Yeah, now I refer, throwing it away, to 'when I was
under psycho-analysis'.

ANNA: The way you refer, throwing it away, to 'when I was
a car salesman', which you were for a week.

DAVE: Why do you always have to cut me down to size?

ANNA: So, how many times did you go?

DAVE: Twice.

[ANNA laughs.]

DAVE: The first interview was already not a success. Now, doc,
I said. I have no wish to discuss my childhood. There is no

point whatever in discussing it. I want to know how to live
my life, doc. I don't want you to sit there, nodding while I
talk. I want your advice, I said. After all, doc, I said, you're
an educated man, Eton and Oxford, so you told me – throwing it away, of course. So pass on the message, doc, pass it
on.

[ANNA *rolls on the carpet, laughing.*]

DAVE: It was no laughing matter. I talked for one hour by the
clock, begging and pleading for the favour of one construc-
tive word from him. But he merely sat like this, and then
he said: 'I'll see you next Thursday, at five o'clock precisely.'
I said, it was no laughing matter – for a whole week I was
in a trance, waiting for the ultimate revelation – you know
how we all live, waiting for that revelation? Then I danced
up to his room and lay on to his couch and lay waiting. He
said not a word. Finally I said don't think I'm resisting you,
doc, please don't think it. Talk doc, I said. Give. Let yourself
go. Then the hour was nearly up. I may say, I'd given him
a thumb-nail sketch of my life previously. He spoke at last:
'Tell me, Mr Miller, how many jobs did you say you had
had?' My God, doc, I said, nearly falling over myself in my
eagerness to oblige, if I knew, I'd tell you. 'You would
admit,' he said at last, 'that the pattern of your life shows,
ho, hum, ha, a certain instability?' My God, yes, doc, I said,
panting at his feet, that's it, you're on to it, hold fast to it
doc, that's the word, instability. Now give doc, give. Tell
me, why is it that a fine upstanding American boy like me,
with all the advantages our rich country gives its citizens,
why should I be in such trouble. And why should so many
of us be in such trouble – I'm not an American for nothing,
I'm socially minded, doc. Why are there so many of us in
such trouble? Tell me doc. Give. And why should you, Dr
Melville Cooper-Anstey, citizen of England, be sitting in that
chair, in a position to dish out advice and comfort? Of course
I know that you got all wrapped up in this thing because
you, uh, kind of like people, doc, but after all, to kinda like
people doc, puts you in a pretty privileged class for a start –

so few citizens can afford to really kinda like people So tell
me doc, tell me . . .

ANNA: Well don't shout at me, I'm not Dr Melville Cooper-
Anstey.

DAVE: You listen just like him – judging. In possession of some
truth that's denied to me.

ANNA: I've always got to be the enemy. You've got to have
an enemy . . .

DAVE: You're right. I've got to have an enemy. Why not? I'm
not going to love my brother as myself if he's not worth it.
Nor my sister, if it comes to that – where was I?

ANNA: Kinda liking people.

DAVE: There was a sort of thoughtful pause. I waited, biting
my nails. Then he said, or drawled. 'Tell me, just at random
now, is there any thing or event or happening that has seemed
to you significant. Just to give us something to get our teeth
into, Mr Miller?' Well, doc, I said, just at random, and picking a significant moment from a life full of significant
moments, and on principle at that – latch on to that doc, it's
important in our case, that my life has been uninterruptedly
full of significant moments . . . but has yours doc? I want to
know? We should talk as equals doc, has your life been as
full as mine of significant moments?

ANNA: Dave, stop boasting.

DAVE: Hell, Anna. If you love me, it's because I lived that
way, Well? And so. But to pull just one little cat or kitten
out of the bag, doc, I would say it was the moment I woke
beside a waitress in Minnesota, and she said to me in her
sweet measured voice: 'Honey you're nuts. Did you know
that?' . . . Well, to tell the truth, no, I hadn't known it. Light
flooded in on me. I've been living with it ever since. And
so. I was all fixed up to see one of your opposite numbers
in the States, my great country, that was in LA, California,
where I happened to be at the time, writing scripts for our
film industry. Then I heard he was a stool pigeon for the
FBI. No, don't look like that doc, don't – very distasteful,
I'll admit, but the world's a rough place. Half his patients
were int-ell-ectuals, and Reds and Pinks, since intellectuals

so often tend to be, and after every couch session, he was moseying off to the FBI with information. Now, doc, here's an American and essentially socially-minded, I want an answer, in this great country, England, I can come to you with perfect confidence that you won't go trotting off to the MI5, to inform them that during my communist period I was a communist. That is, before I was expelled from that institution for hinting that Stalin had his weak moments. I tend to shoot off my mouth, doc. A weakness, I know, but I know that you won't, and that gives me a profound feeling of security.

ANNA: Dave, you're nuts.

DAVE: So said the waitress in Minnesota. Say it often enough and I'll believe it.

ANNA: So what did Dr Cooper-Anstey say?

DAVE: He lightly, oh so lightly, touched his fingertips together, and he drawled: 'Tell me Mr Miller, how many women have you had?'

[ANNA *laughs*.]

DAVE: Hey doc, I said, I was talking seriously. I was talking about the comparative states of liberty in my country and in yours. He said: 'Mr Miller, don't evade my question.'

[ANNA *laughs*.]

DAVE: OK doc, if you're going to be a small-minded . . . but let's leave the statistics, doc. I'm pretty well schooled in this psycho-analysis bit, I said, all my fine stable well integrated friends have been through your mill. And so I know that if I pulled out a notebook full of statistics, you'd think I was pretty sick – you may think it careless of me, doc, but I don't know how many women I've had. But Mr Miller, he drawled, you must have some idea? Well, at this point I see that this particular morale-builder is not for me. Tell me, Dr Melville Cooper-Anstey, I said, how many women have *you* had?

[ANNA *rolls, laughing*.]

DAVE: Hey, Anna, this is serious girl. A serious matter    hey ho, he was mad, was Dr Melville Cooper-Anstey sore. He sat himself up to his full height, and he told me in tones of severe displeasure, that I was an adolescent. Yeah, doc, I said, we Americans are all children, we're all adolescent, we know that. But I wanted to know – how many women have you had doc? Because we have to talk man to man, doc, adolescent or not. There's got to be some sort of equality around this place, I said. After all, I said, one woman is not like another doc, believe me, if you've slept with one woman you've not slept with them all and don't you think it. And besides, doc, I said, you're an Englishman. That is not without relevance. Because, judging from my researches into this field, Englishmen don't like women very much. So English women complain. So they murmur in the dark night watches with their arms gratefully around the stranger's neck. Now I like women doc, I like them. The point is, do you? He laughed. Like this [DAVE *gives a high whinnying laugh*] But I persisted. I said, doc, do you like your wife? And what is more important, does she like you? Does she, doc? And so.

ANNA: And so?

DAVE: And so he kicked me out, with all the dignity an upperclass Englishman brings to such matters. In tones frozen with good taste, he said, 'Mr Miller, you know how to find your own way out, I think.'

ANNA: It's all very well.

DAVE: [*mimicking her*] It's all very well, don't freeze up on me Anna, I won't have it. [*a pause*] Anna, he did vouchsafe me with two little bits of information from the heights of integration. One. He said I couldn't go on like this. I said, that's right, that's why I've come to you. And two. He said I should get married, have two well-spaced children and a settled job. Ah, doc, now you're at the hub of the thing. What job, I said? Because I'll let you into a secret. What's wrong with all of us is not that our mummies and daddies weren't nice to us it's that we don't believe the work we do is important. Oh, I know I'm earnest, doc, I'm pompous and earnest – but I need work that makes me feel I'm contributing. So doc, give – I'm a man of a hundred talents, none of them outstanding. But I have one thing, doc, just one important thing – if I spend eight hours a day working, I need to know that men, women and children are benefiting by my work. So . . . What job shall I do. Tell me.

ANNA: So?

DAVE: He said I should get any job that would enable me to keep a wife and two children, and in this way I would be integrated into society. [*he flings himself down on the carpet*] Anna, for God's sake, Anna.

ANNA: Don't ask me.

DAVE: Why not? I can't ask Dr Anstey. Because the significant moment I keep coming back to he wouldn't see at all. It wasn't the moment I decided to leave America. I drove right across the States, looking up all my friends, the kids who'd been world-challengers with me. They were all married. Some of them were divorced, of course, but that's merely an incident in the process of being married. They all had houses, cars, jobs, families. They were not pleased to see me – they knew I was still unintegrated. I asked each one a simple question. Hey, man, I said, this great country of ours, it's in no too healthy a state. What are we going to do about it? And do you know what they said?

ANNA: Don't rock the boat.

DAVE: You've got it in one, kid. But I had one ace up my sleeve. There was my old buddy, Jedd. He'll still be right in there, fighting. So I walked into his apartment where he was sitting with his brand new second wife. There was a nervous silence. Then he said: Are you successful yet, Dave? And so I took the first boat over.

ANNA: And the wife and the two well-spaced kids?

DAVE: You know I can't get married. You know that if I could I'd marry you. And perhaps I should marry you. How about it?

ANNA: No. The wedding would be the last I'd see of you – you'd be off across the world like a dog with a fire-cracker tied to its tail.

DAVE: I know. So I can't get married. [*a pause*] Why don't you just trap me into it? Perhaps I need simply to be tied down?

ANNA: No.

DAVE: Why not?

ANNA: Any man I have stays with me, voluntarily, because he wants to, without ties.

DAVE: Your bloody pride is more important to you than what I need.

ANNA: Don't beat me up.

DAVE: I will if I want. You're my woman so if I feel like beating you up I will. And you can fight back ... Anna what are you being enigmatic about? All the time, there's something in the air, that's not being said. What is it?

ANNA: Not being said, I keep trying. Don't you really know.

DAVE [in a panic]: No. What?

ANNA: If I told you, you'd say I was just imagining it. All right, I'll try again, Janet Stevens.

DAVE [furious]: You're a monomaniac. Janet Stevens. Do you imagine that a nice little middle-class girl, whose poppa's sort of sub-manager for an insurance company, do you imagine she can mean anything to me?

ANNA: Oh my God, Dave.

DAVE: You're crazy. It's you that's crazy.

ANNA: Dave, while you're banging and crashing about the world, playing this role and that role, filling your life full of significant moments – there are other people in the world ... hell, what's the use of talking to you. [a pause] As a matter of interest, and this is a purely abstract question, suppose you married Janet Stevens, what would you have to do?

DAVE: Anna, are you crazy? Can you see me? God help me, I'm a member of that ever-increasing and honourable company, the world's ex-patriates. Like you, Anna.

ANNA: Oh, all right.

DAVE: How the hell could I marry her? She wouldn't understand a word I ever said, for a start.

ANNA: Oh all right.

DAVE: 'There's no point at all in discussing it.'

ANNA: None at all.

DAVE: I said to Dr Melville Cooper-Anstey: This society you

want me to be integrated with, do you approve of it? If you
don't, what are you doing, sitting there with those big black
scissors cutting people into shapes to fit it? Well, doc, I'll tell
you something, I don't approve of society, it stinks. I don't
want to fit into it, I want society to fit itself to me – I'll
make a deal with you, doc, I'll come and lie on this comfortable couch of yours, Tuesdays and Fridays from 2 to 3 for
seven years, on condition that at the end of that time society
is a place fit for Dave Miller to live in. How's that for
a proposition doc? Because of course that means you'll
have to join the Dave Miller fraternity for changing the
world. You join my organization and I'll join yours. [*he
turns on* ANNA] Hey, Anna, don't just lie there, reserving
judgment.

ANNA: I didn't say a word.

DAVE: You never have to. You're like Dr Melville Cooper-
Anstey – you put your spiritual fingertips together and purse
your lips.

ANNA [*furious*]: Dave do you know something – when you
need an enemy, you turn me into a kind of – lady welfare
worker. Who was the great enemy of your childhood? The
lady welfare worker. [*jumping up – in Australian*] I'm Anna
MacClure the daughter of a second-hand car dealer. My
grand-father was a horse-doctor. My great-grand-father was a
stock farmer. And my great-great-grand-father was a convict,
shipped from this our mother country God bless her to popu-
late the outback. I'm the great-great-grand-daughter of a
convict, I'm the aristocracy so don't get at me, Dave Miller,
corner-boy, street-gang-leader – I'm as good as you are, any
day. [*he pulls her down on to the carpet, she pushes his hands
away*] No. I told you, no.

DAVE [*swinging her round to sit by him. His arms round her*]: OK
then baby, we don't have to make love. Like hell we don't.
OK sit quiet and hold my hand. Do you love me, Anna?

ANNA: Love you? You are me. [*mocking*] You are the flame,
the promise and the enchantment. You are for me –
what Janet Stevens is for you. [*she laughs*] Imagine it Dave
Miller, for you the flame is embodied in a succession

of well-conducted young ladies, each one more banal than the last. For me – it's you. [*suddenly serious*] You are my soul.

DAVE [*holding her down beside him*]: If I'm your soul, then surely it's in order to sit beside me?

[*They sit, arms round each other,* ANNA'S *head on his shoulder.*]

ANNA: I only breathe freely when I'm with you.

DAVE [*complacent*]: I know.

ANNA [*furious*]: What do you mean? I was on the point of getting married.

DAVE: Don't be absurd.

ANNA: What's going to become of us?

DAVE: Perhaps I shall go back to Dr Melville Cooper-Anstey – like hell.

ANNA: It's not fair to take it out of Dr Melville Cooper-Anstey just because he isn't God.

DAVE: Of course it's fair. If God wasn't dead I wouldn't be going to Dr Melville Cooper-Anstey. Perhaps I should wrestle with him – after all, these people have what's the word? Stability.

ANNA: Stability. Security. Safety.

DAVE: You were born with one skin more than I have.

ANNA [*mocking*]: But I come from a stable home.

DAVE: Dr Melville Cooper-Anstey said to me: 'Mr Miller, your trouble is, you come from a broken home.' But doc, I said, my home wasn't broken – my parents were both union organizers. He winced. A look of distaste settled around his long sensitive nose. He fought for the right comment. At last it came: 'Really?' he said. Yeah, really, I said. My parents were professional union organisers.

ANNA [*being* DR MELVILLE COOPER-ANSTEY]: Union organizers, Mr Miller?

DAVE: That's right, doc, it's true that my childhood was spent hither and thither as you might say, but it was in a good cause. My mother was usually organizing a picket line in Detroit while my father was organizing a strike in Pittsburgh.

ANNA: Really, Mr Miller.

DAVE: But doc, it was the late 'twenties and early 'thirties — people were hungry, they were out of work.

ANNA: You must stick to the point Mr Miller.

DAVE: But if I spent my time hither and thither it was not because my parents quarrelled. They loved each other.

ANNA: Were you, or were you not, a disturbed child, Mr Miller?

DAVE: The truth compels me to state, I was a disturbed child. But in a good cause. My parents thought the state of the world was more important than me, and they were right, I am on their side. But I never really saw either of them. We scarcely met. So my mother was whichever lady welfare worker that happened to be dealing with the local delinquents at the time, and my father was the anarchists, the Jewish socialist youth, the communists and the Trotskyists. In a word, the radical tradition — oh, don't laugh doc. I don't expect they'll have taught you about the radical tradition in Oxford, England, but it stood for something. And it will again — it stood for the great dream — that life can be noble and beautiful and dignified.

ANNA: And what did he say?

DAVE: He said I was an adolescent. Doc, I said, my childhood was disturbed — by the great dream — and if yours was not, perhaps after all you had the worst of it.

ANNA: You are evading the issue, Mr Miller.

DAVE: But you're all right, you have stability — Anna, you didn't come from a broken home.

ANNA: No, I come from a well-integrated, typical stable marriage.

DAVE: Then tell me Anna, tell me about stable and well-integrated marriage.

ANNA [standing up and remembering. She shudders]: My mother wanted to be a great pianist. Oh she was not without talent. She played at a concert in Brisbane once — that was the high point of her life. That night she met my father. They married. She never opened the piano after I was born. My father never earned as much money as he thought life owed him — for some reason, the second-hand cars had a spite on him.

My mother got more and more garrulous. In a word, she
was a nag. My father got more and more silent. But he used
to confide in me. He used to tell me what his dreams had
been when he was a young man. Oh yes, he was a world-
changer too, before he married.

DAVE: All young men are world-changers, before they marry.

ANNA: OK. It's not my fault . . .

[*They look at each other.* DAVE *leaps up, switches out the light.*
DAVE *stands across from* ANNA, *in a hunched, defeated pose.*
ANNA *has her hands on her hips, a scold.*]

ANNA: Yes, Mr MacClure, you said that last month – but how
am I going to pay the bill from the store, tell me that?

DAVE [*in Australian*]: A man came in today, he said he might
buy that Ford.

ANNA: Might buy! Might buy! And I promised Anna a new
coat, I promised her, this month, a new coat.

DAVE: Then Anna can do without, it won't hurt her.

ANNA: That's just like you – you always say next month, next
month things will be better – and how about the boy, how
can we pay his fees, we promised him this year . . .

DAVE: Ah, shut up. [*shouting*] Shut up. I said. Shut up . . .

[*He turns away, hunched up.*]

ANNA [*speaking aloud the monologue of her mother's thoughts*]: Yes,
that's how I spend my life, pinching and saving – all day,
cooking and preserving, and making clothes for the kids,
that's all I ever do, I never even get a holiday. And it's for
a man who doesn't even know I'm here – well, if he had
to do without me, he'd know what I've done for him. He'd
value me if he had to do without me – if I left him, he'd
know, soon enough. There's Mr Jones from the store; he's
a soft spot for me, trying to kiss me when there's no one
there but us two, yes, I'd just have to lift my finger and Mr
Jones would take me away – I didn't lack for men before I
married – they came running when I smiled. Ah God in
heaven, if I hadn't married this good-for-nothing here, I'd
be a great pianist, I'd know all the golden cities of the world

– Paris, Rome, London, I'd know the great world, and here I am, stuck in a dump like this, with two ungrateful kids and a no-good husband . . .

DAVE [*speaking aloud* MR MACCLURE'S *thoughts*]: Well what the hell does she want – I wouldn't be here in this dump at all if it wasn't for her; does she think that's all I'm fit for, selling old cars, to keep food and clothes in the home? Why, if I hadn't married her, I'd be free to go where I liked – she sees me as a convenience to get money to keep her and her kids, that's all she cares about, the kids, she doesn't care for me. Without her I'd be off across the world – the world's a big place I'd be free to do what I liked – and the women, yes, the women, why, she doesn't regard me, but only last week, Mrs Jones was giving me the glad eye from behind the counter when her old man wasn't looking – yes, she'd better watch out, she'd miss me right enough if I left her . . .

ANNA [*as* ANNA]: A typical well-integrated marriage. [*as her* MOTHER]: Mr MacClure, are you listening to me?

DAVE [*as* MR MACCLURE]: Yes, dear.

ANNA [*going to him, wistful*]: You're not sorry you married me?

DAVE: No dear, I'm not sorry I married you.

[*They smile at each other, ironical.*]

ANNA [*as* ANNA]: The highest emotion they ever knew was a kind of ironical compassion – the compassion of one prisoner for another . . . [*as her* MOTHER] There's the children, dear. They are both fine kids, both of them.

DAVE: Yes, dear, they're both fine kids. [*patting her*] There, there dear, it's all right, don't worry dear.

ANNA [*as* ANNA]: That's how it was. And when I was nine years old I looked at that good fine stable marriage and at the marriages of our friends and neighbours and I swore, to the God I already did not believe in, God, I said, God, if I go down in loneliness and misery, if I die alone somewhere in a furnished room in a lonely city that doesn't know me – I'll do that sooner than marry as my father and mother were married. I'll have the truth with the man I'm with or I'll have nothing. [*shuddering*] Nothing.

DAVE: Hey – Anna!

[*He switches on the lights, fast. Goes to her.*]

DAVE [*gently*]: Perhaps the irony was the truth.

ANNA: No, no, no. It was *not*.

DAVE [*laughing at her, but gently*]: You're a romantic, Anna Freeman. You're an adolescent.

ANNA: Yes, I'm an adolescent. And that's how I'm going to stay. Anything, anything rather than the man and woman, the jailed and the jailer, living together, talking to themselves, and wondering what happened that made them strangers. I won't, I'll die alone first. And I shall. I shall.

DAVE [*holding her*]: Hey, Anna, Anna. [*gently laughing*] You know what Dr Melville Cooper-Anstey would say to that?

ANNA: Yes.

DAVE: And what all the welfare workers would say?

ANNA: Yes.

DAVE: And what all the priests would say?

ANNA: Yes.

DAVE: And what the politicians would say?

ANNA: Yes. [*she tears herself from him*] Don't rock the boat.

DAVE: [*taking her up*]: Don't rock the boat. [*he switches off the lights*]

[*They look at each other, beginning to laugh. The following sequence, while they throw slogans, or newspaper headlines at each other should be played with enjoyment, on the move, trying to out-cap each other.*]

ANNA: Don't rock the boat – work.

DAVE: Produce goods and children for the State.

ANNA: Marry young.

DAVE: The unit of society is a stable marriage.

ANNA: The unit of a healthy society is a well-integrated family.

DAVE: Earn money.

ANNA: Remember the first and worst sin is poverty.

DAVE: The first and best virtue is to own a comfortable home full of labour-saving devices.

ANNA: If you have too much leisure, there are football matches, the pools and television.

DAVE: If you still have too much leisure be careful not to spend it in ways that might rock the boat.

ANNA: Don't rock the boat – society might have its minor imperfections, but they are nothing very serious.

DAVE: Don't dream of anything better – dreams are by definition neurotic.

ANNA: If you are dissatisfied with society, you are by definition unstable.

DAVE: If your soul doesn't fit into the patterns laid down for you –

ANNA: Kill yourself, but don't rock the boat.

DAVE: Be integrated.

ANNA: Be stable.

DAVE: Be secure.

ANNA: Be integrated or –

DAVE: ⎫
ANNA: ⎭ Die! Die! Die!

DAVE: The trouble with you, Anna, is that you exaggerate everything.

ANNA: The trouble with you Dave, is that you have no sense of proportion.

DAVE: Proportion. I have no sense of proportion. I must scale myself down . . . I have spent my whole life on the move . . . I've spent my youth on the move across the continent and back again – from New York to Pittsburgh, from Pittsburgh to Chicago, from Chicago . . . [*by now he is almost dancing his remembering*] . . . across the great plains of the Middle West to Salt Lake City and the Rocky Mountains, and down to the sea again at San Francisco. Then back again, again, again, from West to East, from North to South, from Dakota to Mexico and back again . . . and sometimes, just sometimes, when I've driven twelve hours at a stretch with the road rolling up behind me like a carpet, sometimes I've reached it, sometimes I've reached what I'm needing – my head rests on the Golden Gates, with one hand I touch Phoenix, Arizona, and with the other I hold Minneapolis,

and my feet straddle from Maine in the Florida Keys. And
under me America rocks, America rocks – like a woman.

ANNA: Or like the waitress from Minnesota.

DAVE: Ah, Jesus!

ANNA: You are maladjusted Mr Miller!

DAVE: But you aren't, do tell me how you do it!

ANNA: Now when I can't breathe any more I shut my eyes
and I walk out into the sun – I stand on a ridge of high
country and look out over leagues and leagues of – emptiness.
Then I bend down and pick up a handful of red dust, a
handful of red dust and I smell it. It smells of sunlight.

DAVE: Of sunlight.

ANNA: I tell you, if I lived in this bloody mildewed little country
for seven times seven years, my flesh would be sunlight.
From here to here, sunlight.

DAVE: You're neurotic, Anna, you've got to face up to it.

ANNA: But you're all right, you're going to settle in a split-level
house with a stable wife and two children.

DAVE [pulling ANNA to the front of the stage and pointing over and
down into the house]: Poke that little nose of yours over your
safe white cliffs and look down – see all those strange coloured
fish down there – not cod, and halibut and Dover sole and
good British herring, but the poisonous coloured fish of
Paradise.

ANNA: Cod. Halibut. Dover Sole. Good British herring.

DAVE: Ah, Jesus, you've got the soul of a little housewife from
Brixton.

ANNA [leaping up and switching on the lights]: Or from Philadelphia. Well let me tell you Dave Miller, any little housewife
from Brixton or Philadelphia could tell you what's wrong
with you.

DAVE [mocking]: Tell me baby.

ANNA: You are America, the America you've sold your soul
to – do you know what she is?

DAVE [mocking]: No baby, tell me what she is.

ANNA: She's that terrible woman in your comic papers – a
great masculine broad-shouldered narrow-hipped black-
booted blonde beastess, with a whip in one hand and a

revolver in the other. And that's why you're running, she's after you, Dave Miller, as she's after every male American I've ever met. I bet you even see the Statue of Liberty with great black thigh-boots and a pencilled moustache – the frigid tyrant, the frigid goddess.

DAVE [*mocking*]: But she's never frigid for me, baby. [*he does his little mocking dance*]

ANNA: God's gift to women, Dave Miller.

DAVE: That's right, that's right baby.

ANNA: And have you ever thought what happens to them – the waitress in Minnesota, the farmer's wife in Nebraska, the club-hostess in Detroit? Dave Miller descends for one night, a gift from God, and leaves the next day. 'Boo-hoo, boo-hoo,' she cries, 'stay with me baby.' 'I can't baby, my destiny waits' – your destiny being the waitress in the next drive-in café. [*she is now dancing around him*] And why don't you stay, or don't you know? It's because you're scared. Because if you stay, she might turn into the jackbooted whip-handling tyrant.

DAVE: No. I'm not going to take the responsibility for you. That's what you want, like every woman I've ever known. That I should say, I love you baby and . . .

ANNA: I love you, Anna Freeman.

DAVE: I love you, honey.

ANNA: I love you, Anna Freeman.

DAVE: I love you, doll.

ANNA: I love you, Anna Freeman.

DAVE: I love you – but that's the signal for you to curl up and resign your soul to me. You want me to be responsible for you.

ANNA: You'll never be responsible for anyone. [*flat*] One day you'll learn that when you say I love you baby it means something.

DAVE: Well, everything's running true to form – I haven't been back a couple of hours but the knives are out and the tom-toms beating for the sex-war.

ANNA: It's the only clean war left. It's the only war that won't destroy us all. That's why we are fighting it.

DAVE: Sometimes I think you really hate me, Anna.

ANNA [mocking]: Really? Sometimes I think I've never hated anyone so much in all my life. A good clean emotion hate is. I hate you.

DAVE: Good, then I hate you.

ANNA: Good, then get out, go away. [She wheels to the window, looks out. He goes to where his duffle bag is, picks it up, drops it, and in the same circling movement turns to face her as she says] I hate you because you never let me rest.

DAVE: So love is rest? The cosy corner, the little nook?

ANNA: Sometimes it ought to be.

DAVE: Sometimes it is.

ANNA: Ha! With you! You exhaust me. You take me to every extreme, all the time, I'm never allowed any half-measures.

DAVE: You haven't got any.

ANNA: Ah, hell. [she flings her shoes at him, one after the other. He dodges them, jumps to the bed, crouches on it, patting it]

DAVE: Truce, baby, truce . . .

ANNA [mocking him]: You're going to love me, baby, warm-hearted and sweet? Oh you're a good lay baby, I'd never say you weren't.

[The sound of screechings and fighting from the street. ANNA is about to slam the window down, stops on a look from DAVE.]

ANNA: Last night the four of them were scratching each other and pulling each other's hair while a group of fly-by-night men stood and watched and laughed their heads off. Nothing funnier, is there, than women fighting?

DAVE: Sure, breaks up the trade union for a bit . . . [this is black and aggressive – she reacts away from him. He looks at her, grimaces] Hell, Anna.

[He goes fast to the mirror, studies the black cloth.]

DAVE: What's the pall for?

ANNA: I don't like my face.

DAVE: Why not?

ANNA: It wears too well.

DAVE: You must be hard-up for complaints against life . . .

[*looking closely at her*] You really are in pieces, aren't you? You mean you went out and bought this specially?

ANNA: That's right.

DAVE: Uh-huh — when?

ANNA: When we quarrelled last time — finally, if you remember?

DAVE: Uh-huh. Why really, come clean?

ANNA: It would seem to suit my situation.

DAVE: Uh-huh . . . [*he suddenly whips off the cloth and drapes it round his shoulders like a kind of jaunty cloak, or cape. Talking into the mirror, in angry, mocking self-parody*] Hey there, Dave Miller, is that you, man? [*in a Southern accent*] Yes, Ma'am, and you have a pretty place around here. Mind if I stay a-while? Yeah, I sure do like your way of doing things . . . [*accent of the Mid-West*] Hi, babe, and what've you got fixed for tonight? Yes, this is the prettiest place I've seen for many a day . . . [*in English*] Why, hullo, how are you? [*he crashes his fist into the mirror*]

[ANNA, *watching him, slowly comes from window as he talks, first crouches on the carpet, then collapses face down — she puts her hands over her ears, then takes them away.*]

DAVE [*into mirror*]: Dave Miller? David Abraham Miller? No reply. No one at home. Anna, do you know what I'm scared of? One of these fine days I'll look in the glass, expecting to see a fine earnest ethical young . . . and there'll be nothing there. Then, slowly, a small dark stain will appear on the glass, it will slowly take form and . . . Anna, I want to be a good man. I want to be a good man.

ANNA [*for herself*]: I know.

[*But he has already recovered. He comes to her, pulls her up to sit by him.*]

DAVE: If that God of theirs ever dishes out any medals to us, what'll it be for?

ANNA: No medals for us.

DAVE: Yes, for trying. For going on. For keeping the doors open.

ANNA: Open for *what?*

DAVE: You know. Because if there's anything new in the world anywhere, any new thought, or new way of living, we'll be ready to hear the first whisper of it. When Dr Melville Cooper-Anstey, imagines God, how does he imagine him?

ANNA: As Dr Melville Cooper-Anstey, two sizes larger.

DAVE: But we've got to do better. Anna look — the walls are down, and anyone or anything can come in. Now imagine off the street comes an entirely new and beautiful phenomenon, a new human being.

ANNA: Jewish boy — you're a good Jewish boy after all waiting for the Messiah.

DAVE: That's what everyone's waiting for, even if they don't know it — something new to be born. Anna, supposing superman walked in now off the street, how would you imagine him?

ANNA: Superwoman.

DAVE: Oh OK.

ANNA [*in despair*]: Me.

DAVE: I know. I know it. Me too. I sit and think and think — because if we don't know what we want to grow into, how can we shape ourselves better? So I concentrate until my brain is sizzling, and who comes in through the door — me!

ANNA: Just once it wasn't me.

DAVE [*excited*]: Who?

ANNA: I was sitting here, like this. I was thinking — if we can't breed something better than we are, we've had it, the human race has had it. And then, suddenly . . .

DAVE: What?

ANNA: He walked in, twitching his tail. An enormous, glossy padding tiger. The thing was, I wasn't at all surprised. Well tiger, I said, and who do you belong to?

DAVE [*furious*]: Anna, a tiger walks in here, and all you can say is, wild beast, whose label is around your neck?

ANNA: I thought you wanted to *know.*

DAVE: Go on.

ANNA: The tiger came straight towards me. Hullo tiger, I said, have you escaped from the zoo?

DAVE [*mocking*]: Of *course* he's escaped from the zoo. He couldn't be a wild tiger, could he?

ANNA [*she kneels, talking to the tiger*]: Tiger, tiger, come here. [*she fondles the tiger*] Tiger, tiger — The tiger purred so loud that the sound drowned the noise of the traffic. And then suddenly — [ANNA *starts back, clutching at her arms.*] He lashed out, I was covered with blood. Tiger, I said, what's that for . . . he backed away, snarling.

[ANNA *is now on her feet, after the tiger.*]

DAVE [*very excited*]: Yeah. That's it. That's it. That's it.

ANNA: He jumped on to my bed and crouched there, lashing his tail. But tiger, I said, I haven't done anything to you, have I?

DAVE [*furious*]: Why didn't you offer him a saucer of milk? Kitty, kitty, have a nice saucer of milk?

ANNA [*beside the bed, trying to hold the tiger*]: Tiger, don't go away. But he stared and he glared, and then he was off — down he leaped and out into the street, and off he padded with his yellow eyes gleaming into the shadows of Earls Court. Then I heard the keepers shouting after him and wheeling along a great cage . . . [*She comes back opposite* DAVE.] That was the best I could do. I tried hard, but that was the best — a tiger. And I'm covered with scars.

DAVE [*gently*]: Anna.

[*They kneel, foreheads touching, hands together.*]
[*The telephone starts ringing.*]

DAVE: Answer it.

ANNA: No.

DAVE: Is it Tom?

ANNA: Of course it isn't Tom.

DAVE: Then who?

ANNA: Don't you really know?

[*She goes to answer telephone, it stops ringing. She stands a moment. Then turns to him, fast.*]

ANNA: Love me Dave, Love me Dave. Now.

[DAVE *rolls her on to the carpet. They roll over and over together. Suddenly she breaks free and begins to laugh.*]

DAVE: What's so funny?

ANNA [*kneeling up, mocking*]: I'll tell you what's funny, Dave Miller. We sit here, tearing ourselves to bits trying to imagine something beautiful and new – but suppose the future is a nice little American college girl all hygienic and virginal and respectable with a baby in her arms. Suppose the baby is what we're waiting for – a nice, well-fed, well-educated, psycho-analysed superman . . .

DAVE: Anna, please stop it.

ANNA: But imagine. Anything can come in – tigers, unicorns, monsters, the human being so beautiful he will send all of us into the dust-can. But what does come in is a nice, anxious little girl from Philadelphia.

DAVE: Well Anna?

ANNA: Well Dave?

[*A fresh burst of fighting from the street.* ANNA *moves to shut the window,* DAVE *holds her.*]

DAVE: I'm surprised I have to tell you that anything you shut out because you're scared of it becomes more dangerous.

ANNA: Yes, but I've lived longer than you, and I'm tired.

DAVE: That's a terrible thing to say.

ANNA: I daresay it is.

## END OF ACT TWO

# Act Three

ANNA *and* DAVE *in the same positions as at the end of Act Two —
no time has passed.*

ANNA: Yes, I daresay it is.

[*She goes to the light, switches it on, the room is closed in.*]

ANNA [*as she switches on the light*]: I must be mad. I keep trying
to forget it's all over. But it is.

[*From the moment* ANNA *says 'It's all over' it is as if she has
turned a switch inside herself. She is going inside herself: she has
in fact 'frozen up on him'. This is from self-protection, and* DAVE
*knows it. Of course he knows by now, or half-knows, and still
won't admit to himself, about* JANET. *But he is trying to get
through to* ANNA. *He really can't stand it when she freezes up on
him. From now until when Mary comes in should be played fast,
wild, angry, mocking: they circle around each other, they do not
touch each other.*]

[ANNA *goes straight from the light switch to the record-player, puts
on 'I'm on My Way', goes to the bottom of her bed, where she
kneels, and shuts Dave out by pretending to work on something.*]

DAVE [*shouting across music*]: Anna. I could kill you. [*as she ignores
him*] . . . come clean, what have you been really doing in
the last weeks to get yourself into such a state?

ANNA [*shouting*]: I've been unhappy, I've been so unhappy I
could have died.

DAVE: Ah come on, baby.

ANNA: But I can't say that, can I? To say, You made me
unhappy, is to unfairly curtail your freedom?

DAVE: But why the hell do you have to be unhappy?

ANNA: Oh quite so. But I didn't say it. I've been sitting here, calm as a rock, playing 'I'm on My Way.'

DAVE: Why?

ANNA: It would seem I have the soul of a negro singer.

DAVE: Oh Christ. [*He turns off the record player.*]

ANNA [*too late*]: Leave it on.

DAVE: No, I want to talk.

ANNA: All right, talk. [*He bangs his fist against the wall.*] Or shall I ask you what you've been doing in the last few weeks to get yourself into such a state?

[*A silence.*]

ANNA: Well, talk. [*conversational*] Strange, isn't it how the soul of Western man — what may be referred to, loosely, as the soul of Western man, is expressed by negro folk music and the dark rhythms of the . . . [DAVE *leaps up, he begins banging with his fists against the wall.*] I'm thinking of writing a very profound article about the soul of Western man as expressed by . . .

DAVE [*banging with his fists*]: Shut up.

ANNA: I'm *talking*. Looked at objectively — yes objectively is certainly the word I'm looking for — what could be more remarkable than the fact that the soul of Western man . . .

DAVE [*turning on her*]: You have also, since I saw you last, been engaged to marry Tom Lattimer.

ANNA: Don't tell me you suddenly care?

DAVE: I'm curious.

ANNA [*mocking*]: I was in lurve. Like you were.

DAVE: You were going to settle down?

ANNA: That's right, I decided it was time to settle *down*.

DAVE: If you're going to get married you might at least get married on some sort of a level.

ANNA: But Dave, the phrase is, settle *down*. [*she bends over, holds her hand a few inches from the floor*] It is no accident, surely, that the phrase is settle *down*. [DAVE *stands watching her, banging the side of his fist against the wall.*] I'm thinking of writing a short, pithy, but nevertheless profoundly profound article on the unconscious attitude to marriage revealed in our culture by the phrase settle *down*.

[DAVE *lets his fist drop. Leans casually against the wall, watches her ironically.*]

DAVE: Anna, I know you too well.

ANNA: An article summing up — how shall I put it — the contemporary *reality*.

DAVE: I know you too well.

ANNA: But it seems, not well enough . . . We're through Dave Miller. We're washed up. We're broken off. We're finished.

DAVE [*with simplicity*]: But Anna, you love me.

ANNA: It would seem there are more important things than love.

DAVE [*angry*]: Lust?

ANNA: Lust? What's that? Why is it I can say anything complicated to you but never anything simple? I can't say — you made me unhappy. I can't say — are you sure you're not making someone else unhappy. So how shall I put it? Well, it has just occurred to me in the last five minutes that when Prometheus was in his cradle it was probably rocked by the well-manicured hand of some stupid little goose whose highest thought was that the thatch on her hut should be better plaited than the thatch on her neighbour's hut. Well? Is that indirect enough? After all, it is the essence of the myth that the miraculous baby should not be recognized. And so we are both playing our parts nicely. You because you're convinced it can't happen to *you*. Me because I can't bear to think about it.

DAVE: Anna, you haven't let that oaf Tom Lattimer make you pregnant.

ANNA: Oh my God. No. I haven't. No dear Dave, I'm not pregnant. But perhaps I should be?

DAVE: OK Anna, I'm sorry. I'm sorry I made you unhappy. But — well, here I am Anna.

ANNA: Yes, here you are. [*in pain*] Dave, you have no right, you have no right . . . you're a very careless person, Dave . . . [*She gets off the bed and goes to the window.*] What's the

use of talking of rights and wrongs? Or of right or wrong?
OK, it's a jungle. Anything goes. I should have let myself
get pregnant. One catches a man by getting pregnant. People
like you and me make life too complicated. Back to reality.
[looking down] My God, that poor fool is still down there.

DAVE: Anna, don't freeze up on me.

ANNA: You want to know what I've been doing? Well I've
been standing here at night looking into the street and trying
not to think about what you've been doing. I've been standing here. At about eleven at night the law and the order
dissolve. The girls stand at their window there, kissing or
quarrelling as the case might be, in between customers. The
wolves prowl along the street. Gangs of kids rush by, living
in some frightened lonely violent world that they think we
don't understand – ha! So they think we don't understand
what's driving them crazy? Old people living alone go creeping home, alone. The women who live alone, after an hour
of talking to strangers in a pub, go home, alone. And sometimes a married couple or lovers – and they can't wait to get
inside, behind the walls, they can't wait to lock the doors
against this terrible city. And they're right.

DAVE: They're not right.

ANNA: Put your arms around one other human being, and let
the rest of the world go hang – the world is terrifying, so
shut it out. That's what people are doing everywhere, and
perhaps they are right.

DAVE: Anna, say it!

ANNA: All right. You're an egotist, and egotists can never bear
the thought of a new generation. That's all. And I'm an
egotist and what I call my self-respect is more important to
me than anything else. And that's all. There's nothing new
in it. There's nothing new anywhere. I shall die of boredom.
Sometimes at night I look out into the street and I imagine
that somewhere is a quiet room, and in the room is a man
or a woman, thinking. And quite soon there will be a small
new book – a book of one page perhaps, and on the page
one small new thought. And we'll all read it and shout: Yes,
yes, that's it.

DAVE: Such as?

ANNA [*mocking*]: We must love one another or die, something new like that.

DAVE: Something new like that.

ANNA: But of course it wouldn't be that at all. It would probably turn out to be a new manifesto headed: Six new rules for egotists, or How to eat your cake and have it.

DAVE: Anna, stop beating us up.

ANNA: Ah *hell*.

[DAVE *puts out a hand to her, drops it on her look.*]

DAVE: OK, Anna, have it your way ... You're not even interested in what I've been doing since I saw you? You haven't even asked.

ANNA: The subject, I thought, had been touched on.

DAVE: No, honey, I was being serious. Work, I mean work. I've been working. [*mocking himself*] I've been writing a sociological-type article about Britain.

ANNA: So that is what you've been doing for the last week. *We* were wondering.

DAVE [*acknowledging the 'we'*]: OK Anna, OK, OK.

ANNA: What am I going to be without you? I get so lonely without you.

DAVE: But baby, I'm here. [*at her look*] OK Anna. OK.

ANNA: All right, Dave. But all the same ... I sometimes think if my skin were taken off I'd be just one enormous bruise. Yes, that's all I am, just a bruise.

DAVE: Uh-huh.

ANNA: However, comforting myself with my usual sociological-type thought, I don't see how there can be such pain everywhere without something new growing out of it.

DAVE: Uh-huh.

ANNA [*fierce*]: Yes!

DAVE: All the same, you're tough. At a conservative estimate, a hundred times tougher than I am. Why?

ANNA [*mocking*]: Obviously, I'm a woman, everyone knows we are tough.

DAVE: Uh-huh ... I was thinking, when I was away from you,

every time I take a beating it gets harder to stand up after wards. You take punishment and up you get smiling.

ANNA: Oh quite so. Lucky, isn't it?

DAVE: Tell me, when your husband was killed, did it knock you down?

ANNA: Oh of course not, why should it?

DAVE: OK Anna.

ANNA: Everyone knows that when a marriage ends because the husband is killed fighting heroically for his country the marriage is by definition romantic and beautiful. [at his look] All right, I don't choose to remember. [at his look] OK, it was a long time ago.

DAVE: Well then, is it because you've got that kid?

ANNA [irritated]: Is what because I've got that kid. That kid, that kid ... You talk about him as if he were a plant in a pot on the windowsill, or a parcel I've left lying about some-where, instead of what my life has been about.

DAVE: Why take men seriously when you've got a child?

ANNA [ironic]: Ho-ho, I see.

DAVE: All right then, tell me truthfully, tell me straight, baby, none of the propaganda now, what does it really mean to you to have that kid?

ANNA: But why should you be interested, you're not going to have children ...

DAVE: Come on, Anna, you can't have it both ways.

ANNA: No.

DAVE: Why not?

ANNA [angry]: Because I can never say anything I think, I feel – it always ends up with what you think, you feel. My God, Dave, sometimes I feel you like a great black shadow over me I've got to get away from ... oh all right, all right ... [She stands, slowly smiles.]

DAVE: Don't give me that Mona Lisa stuff, I want to know.

ANNA: Well. He sets me free. Yes, that's it, he sets me free.

DAVE: Why, for God's sake, you spend your time in savage domesticity whenever he's within twenty miles of you.

ANNA: Don't you see? He's there. I go into his room when he's asleep to take a good long look at him, because he's too old

now to look at when he's awake, that's already an inter-
ference. So I look at him. He's *there*.

DAVE: He's there.

ANNA: There he is. He's something new. A kind of ray of light
that shoots off into any direction. Or blazes up like a comet
or goes off like a rocket.

DAVE [*angry*]: Oh don't tell me, you mean it gives you a sense
of power — you look at him and you think — I made that.

ANNA: No, that's not it. Well, that's what I said would happen.
You asked, I told you, and you don't believe me.

[*She turns her back on him, goes to window. A long wolf-whistle
from outside. Another.*]

ANNA: Let's ask him up and tell him the facts of life.

DAVE: Not much point if he hasn't got fifty shillings.

ANNA: The State is prosperous. He will have fifty shillings.

DAVE: No, let us preserve romance. Let him dream.

[*Shouting and quarrelling from the street.*]

DAVE [*at window with her*]: There's the police.

ANNA: They're picking up the star-struck hero as well.

DAVE: No mixing of the sexes at the police station so he can
go on dreaming of his loved-one from afar even now.

[*A noise of something falling on the stairs. Voices. Giggling.*]

DAVE: What the hell's that?

ANNA: It's Mary.

DAVE: She's got herself a man? Good for her.

ANNA [*distressed and irritable*]: No, but she's going to get herself
laid. Well that's OK with you isn't it? Nothing wrong with
getting oneself laid, according to you.

DAVE: It might be the beginning of something serious for her.

ANNA: Oh quite so. And when you get yourself laid. [*conver-
sationally and with malice*] It's odd the way the American male
talks of getting himself laid. In the passive. 'I went out and
got myself laid' what a picture — the poor helpless creature,
pursuing his own pure concerns, while the predatory female
creeps up behind him and lays him on his back . . .

DAVE. Don't get at me because you're worried about Mary.

[*He goes over and puts his arm about her. For a moment, she accepts it.*] Who is it?

ANNA: Harry. [MARY *and* HARRY *have arrived outside* ANNA'S *door. Can be seen as two shadows. One shadow goes upstairs. One shadow remains.*] I hope she doesn't come in.

DAVE: But he shouldn't be here if Helen's in a bad way . . . [*as* ANNA *looks at him*] Hell. [*He goes across to the mirror, where he stands grimacing at himself.*]

[MARY *knocks and comes in. She is rather drunk and aggressive.*]

MARY: You're up late aren't you?

ANNA: Have a good time?

MARY: He's quite amusing, Harry. [*She affects a yawn.*] I'm dead. Well, I think I'll pop off to bed. [*looking suspiciously at* ANNA] You weren't waiting up for me, were you?

ANNA [*looking across at* DAVE]: No.

[MARY *sees* DAVE, *who is draping the black cloth across the mirror.*]

MARY: Well, what a stranger. What are you doing? Don't you like the look of yourself?

DAVE: Not very much. Do you?

MARY: I've been talking over old times with Harry.

DAVE: Yes, Anna said.

MARY: I expect you two have been talking over old times too. I must go to bed, I'm dead on my feet. [*There is a noise upstairs.*] [*quickly*] That must be the cat. Have you seen the cat?

ANNA: Yes, I suppose it must.

MARY: I was saying to Anna, only today, I'm getting a proper old maid – if a widow can be an old maid, fussing over a cat, well you'd never believe when you were young what you'll come to.

DAVE: You an old maid – you've got enough spunk for a twenty-year-old.

MARY: Yes, Harry was saying, I wouldn't think you were a day over twenty-five, he said. [*to* DAVE] Did you know my boy was getting married next week?

DAVE: Yes, I heard.

MARY: He's got himself a nice girl. But I can't believe it. It seems only the other day ... [*There is a bang upstairs. A moment later, a loud miaow outside* ANNA'S *door.*] Why, there's my pussy cat. [*Another crash upstairs.*] I must go and see ... [*She scuttles out.* HARRY'S *shadow on the stairs.*] [*putting her head around the door*] Isn't it nice, Harry's decided to pop back for a cup of coffee. [*She shuts the door.*]

[ANNA *and* DAVE, *in silence, opposite each other on the carpet. Dance music starts, soft, upstairs.*]

ANNA: A good lay, with music.

DAVE: Don't, baby. If I was fool enough to marry I'd be like Harry.

ANNA: Yes.

DAVE: Don't hate him.

ANNA: I can make out Harry's case as well as you. He wanted to be a serious writer, but like a thousand others he's got high standards and no talent. So he works on a newspaper he despises. He goes home to a wife who doesn't respect him. So he has to have the little girls to flatter him and make him feel good. OK Dave – but what more do you want? I'll be back on duty by this evening, pouring out sympathy in great wet gobs and I'll go on doing it until he finds another little girl who looks at him with gooey eyes and says: oh Harry, oh Dave, you're so wonderful.

DAVE: It wouldn't do you any harm to indulge in a bit of flattery from time to time.

ANNA: Oh yes it would. I told you, I'm having the truth with a man or nothing. I watch women buttering up their men, anything for a quiet life and despising them while they do it. It makes me sick.

DAVE: Baby, I pray for the day when you flatter me for just ten seconds.

ANNA: Oh go and get it from – Janet.

[MARY *comes in fast, without knocking.*]

MARY [*she is very aggressive*]: Anna, I didn't like your manner just now. Sometimes there is something in your way I don't like at all.

[ANNA *turns away.*]

ANNA: Mary, you're a little high.

MARY: I'm not. I'm not tight at all. I've had practically nothing to drink. And you don't even listen. I'm serious and you're not listening. [*taking hold of Anna*] I'm not going to have it. I'm simply not going to have it.

[HARRY *comes in. He is half drunk.*]

HARRY: Come on, Mary. I thought you were going to make me some coffee. [MARY *bangs ineffectually at* ANNA'S *shoulder with her fist.*] Hey, girls, don't brawl at this time of night.

MARY: I'm not brawling. [*to* DAVE] He's smug too, isn't he. Like Anna. [*to* ANNA] And what about you? This afternoon you were still with Tom and now it's Dave.

HARRY: You're a pair of great girls.

[ANNA *looks in appeal at* DAVE.]

DAVE [*coming gently to support* MARY]: Hey, Mary, come on now.

MARY [*clinging to him*]: I like you Dave. I always did. When people say to me, that crazy Dave, I always say, I like Dave. I mean, it's only the crazy people who understand life when you get down to it . . .

DAVE: That's right, Mary. [*He supports her.*]

[HARRY *comes and attempts to take* MARY'S *arm.* MARY *shakes him off and confronts* ANNA.]

MARY: Well Anna, that's what I wanted to say and I've said it.

[HARRY *is leading* MARY *out.*]

MARY: The point is, what I mean is.

HARRY: You've made your point, come on.

ANNA: See you in the morning, Mary.

MARY: Well I've been meaning to say it and I have.

[HARRY *and* MARY *go out,* HARRY *with a nod and a smile at the other two.*]

DAVE: Anna, she'll have forgotten all about it in the morning.

[*He goes to her. She clings to him.*]

DAVE: And if she hasn't, you'll have to.

ANNA: Oh hell, hell, hell.

DAVE: Yes, I know baby, I know.

ANNA: She's going to wish she were dead tomorrow morning.

DAVE: Well, it's not so terrible. You'll be here and you can pick up the pieces. [*He leads her to the bed, and sits by her, his arm around her.*] That's better. I like looking after you. Let's have six months' peace and quiet. Let's have a truce — what do you say?

[*The telephone rings. They are both tense, listening.* HARRY *comes in.*]

HARRY: Don't you answer your telephone, Anna? What's the matter with you two? [*He goes to the telephone to answer it. Sees their faces, stops.*] I'm a clod. Of course, it's Tom.

ANNA: It isn't Tom.

HARRY: Of course it is. Poor bastard, he's breaking his heart and here you are dallying with Dave.

ANNA: I know it isn't.

DAVE: Never argue with Anna when she's got one of her fits of intuition.

ANNA: Intuition!

HARRY: Mary's passed clean out. Mary's in a bad way tonight. Just my luck. I need someone to be nice to me, and all Mary wants is someone to be nice to her.

ANNA: I hope you were.

HARRY: Of course I was.

ANNA: Why don't you go home to Helen?

HARRY [*bluff*]: It's four in the morning. Did you two fools know it's four in the morning? I'll tell Helen my troubles tomorrow. Anna, don't tell me you're miserable too, [*going to her*] Is that silly bastard Dave playing you up? It's a hell of a life. Now I'll tell you what. I'll pick you up for lunch tomorrow, I mean today, and I'll tell you my troubles and you can tell me yours. [*to* DAVE] You've made Anna unhappy, you clod, you idiot.

ANNA: Oh damn it, if you want to play big Daddy why don't you go home and mop up some of Helen's tears?

HARRY [*bluff*]: I don't have to worry about Helen, I keep telling you.

ANNA: Harry!

HARRY [*to* DAVE, *shouting it*]: Clod. Fool . . . all right, I suppose I've got to go home. But it's not right, Anna. God in his wisdom has ordained that there should be a certain number of understanding women in the world whose task it is to bind up the wounds of warriors like Dave and me. Yes, I'll admit it, it's hard on you but – you're a man's woman Anna, and that means that when we're in trouble you can't be.

ANNA: Thank you, I did understand my role.

[*The telephone rings.*]

HARRY: He's a persistent bugger, isn't he? [*He picks up telephone, shouts into it.*] Well you're not to marry him, Anna. Or anyone. Dave and I won't let you. [*He slams receiver back.*]

ANNA: Go home. Please go home.

HARRY [*for the first time serious*]: Anna, you know something? I'm kind Uncle Harry, the world's soft shoulder for about a thousand people. I make marriages, I patch them up. I give good advice. I dish out aid and comfort. But there's just one person in the world I can't be kind to.

ANNA: Helen's ill.

HARRY: I know she is. I know it. But every time it's the same thing. I go in, full of good intentions – and then something happens. I don't know what gets into me . . . I was looking into the shaving glass this morning, a pretty sight I looked, I was up all last night drinking myself silly because my poppet's getting married. I looked at myself. You silly sod, I said. You're fifty this year, and you're ready to die because of a little girl who . . . you know, Anna, if she wanted me to cut myself into pieces for her I'd do it? And she looked at me yesterday with those pretty little eyes of hers and she said – primly, she said it, though not without kindness – Harry, do you know what's wrong with you? You're at the dangerous age, she said. All men go through it. Oh Christ, Anna, let me take you out and give you a drink tonight. I've got to weep on someone's shoulder. I'd have wept on Mary's, only all she could say was: 'Harry, what's the meaning of life?' She asks me.

ANNA: Anything you like but for God's sake go home now.

HARRY: I'm going. Helen will pretend to be asleep. She never says anything. Well I suppose she's learned there's not much point in her saying anything, poor bitch.

[*He goes.* DAVE *and* ANNA *look at each other.*]

DAVE: OK Anna. Now let's have it.

ANNA [*in cruel parody*]: I'm just a little ordinary girl, what's wrong with that? I want to be married, what's wrong with that? I never loved anyone as I loved Dave . . .

DAVE: No, Anna, not like that.

ANNA [*in* JANET'S *voice, wild with anxiety*]: When I knew I was pregnant I was so happy. Yes I know how it looks, trapping a man, but he said he loved me, he said he loved me. I'm five months' pregnant.

[*She stands waiting.* DAVE *looks at her.*]

ANNA: Well haven't you got anything to say?

DAVE: Did you expect me to fall down at your feet and start grovelling? God Anna, look at you, the mothers of the universe have triumphed, the check's on the table and Dave Miller's got to pay the bill, that's it, isn't it?

[*She says nothing.* DAVE *laughs.*]

ANNA: Funny?

DAVE [*with affection*]: You're funny, Anna.

ANNA: It's not my baby. I'm sorry it isn't. I wasn't so intelligent.

DAVE: That's right. You've never got the manacles on me, but

Janet has. Now I marry Janet and settle down in the insurance business and live happily ever after, is it that? Is that how you see it? If not, this cat and mouse business all evening doesn't make sense.

ANNA: And the baby? Just another little casualty in the sex war? She's a nice respectable middle-class girl, you can't say to her, have an illegitimate baby, it will be an interesting experience for you — you could have said it to me.

DAVE: Very nice, and very respectable.

ANNA: You said you loved her.

DAVE: Extraordinary. You're not at all shocked that she lied to me all along the line?

ANNA: You told her you loved her.

DAVE: I'll admit it's time I learned to define my terms . . . you're worried about Janet's respectability? If the marriage certificate is what is important to her I'll give her one. No problems.

ANNA: No problems!

DAVE: I'll fix it. Anna, you know what? You've been using Janet to break off with me because you haven't the guts to do it for yourself? I don't come through for you so you punish me by marrying me off to Janet Stevens?

ANNA: OK, then why don't you come through for me? Here you are, Dave Miller, lecturing women all the time about how they should live — women should be free, they should be independent, etc., etc. None of these dishonest female ruses. But if that's what you really want what are you doing with Janet Stevens — and all the other Janets? Well? The truth is you can't take us, you can't take me. I go through every kind of bloody misery trying to be what you say you want, but . . .

DAVE: OK, some of the time I can't take you.

ANNA: And what am I supposed to do when you're off with the Janets?

DAVE [with confidence]: Well you can always finally kick me out.

ANNA: And in a few months' time when you've got tired of yourself in the role of a father, there'll be a knock on the door . . . 'Hi, Anna, do you love me? Let's have six months'

peace and quiet, let's have a truce . . .' and so on, and so on,
and so on, and so on . . .

[*The telephone rings.*]

DAVE [*at telephone*]: Hi, Janet. Yeah. OK, baby. OK, I'm on
my way. Don't cry baby. [*He puts down receiver.*]

[*They look at each other.*]

DAVE: Well baby?
ANNA: Well?

[*He goes out. Now* ANNA *has a few moments of indecision, of
unco-ordination. She begins to cry, but at once stops herself. She
goes to the cupboard, brings out Scotch and a glass. She nearly fills
the glass with Scotch. With this in her hand she goes to the mirror,
carefully drapes the black cloth over it. Goes to the carpet, where
she sits as if she were still sitting opposite Dave. The Scotch is on
the carpet beside her. She has not drunk any yet.* ANNA *sits holding
herself together, because if she cracked up now, it would be too
terrible. She rocks herself a little, perhaps, picks a bit of fluff off her
trousers, makes restless, unco-ordinated movements.* MARY *comes
in.*]

MARY: I must have fallen asleep. I don't know what Harry
thought, me falling asleep like that . . . what did you say? I
don't usually . . . Where's Dave?
ANNA: He's gone to get married.
MARY: Oh. Well he was bound to get married some time,
wasn't he?

[*Now she looks closely at* ANNA *for the first time.*]

MARY: I must have been pretty drunk. I still am if it comes to
that.

[*She looks at the glass of Scotch beside Anna, then at the black
cloth over the mirror.*]

MARY: Hadn't you better get up?

[MARY *goes to the mirror, takes off the black cloth and begins to fold it up. She should do this like a housewife folding a tablecloth, very practical.*]

MARY: I suppose some people will never have any more sense than they were born with.

[*She lays down the cloth, folded neatly. Now she comes to Anna, takes up the glass of Scotch, and pours it back into the bottle.*]

MARY: God only knows how I'm going to get myself to work today, but I suppose I shall.

[*She comes and stands over* ANNA. ANNA *slowly picks herself off the floor and goes to the window.*]

MARY: That's right. Anna, have you forgotten your boy'll be home in a few days? [*as* ANNA *responds*] That's right. Well we always say we shouldn't live like this, but we do, don't we, so what's the point . . . [*She is now on her way to the door.*] I was talking to my boy this morning Twenty-four. He knows everything. What I wouldn't give to be back at twenty-four, knowing everything . . .

[MARY *goes out. Now* ANNA *slowly goes towards the bed. As she does so, the city comes up around her, and the curtain comes down.*]

THE END

# THE SINGING DOOR

# CHARACTERS

CHAIRMAN
FIFTH PRECEPT
FOURTH PRECEPT
SECRETARY
GUARDIAN OF THE DOOR
DELEGATES
TWO DISSIDENT DELEGATES
ATTENDANTS
GUARDS
FIRST LOW-LEVELLER
SECOND LOW-LEVELLER
THIRD LOW-LEVELLER
FOURTH LOW-LEVELLER
TWO MEDICAL ASSISTANTS
DOCTOR
ASSISTANT TO GUARDIAN OF THE DOOR
A GROUP OF PEOPLE FROM VARIOUS LEVELS
TWO LATE-COMERS
ASSISTANTS AND HELPERS AT THE ALTAR
TECHNICIAN

# The Singing Door

SCENE: *Is this a cave? If so, it is a cave into which has been fitted technical equipment. Perhaps it is an underground shelter for time of war? At any rate, this place combines a rawness of earth and rock with advanced gadgetry. This last is piled up at centre back in a way which suggests an altar or a sacred place: computer, radio receiving apparatus, television set, electronic devices — any or all of these. None of these things is working. In the middle of this arrangement is set, in the place of honour, an unattached wooden door. Every item is much garlanded and decorated, but the flowers and greenery are artificial. The altar's* ATTENDANTS *are wearing technicians' uniforms. They are in attitudes of worship, telling beads, muttering mantras, and so on.*

*At left is a rough rocky exit into the deeper levels of this underground place.*

*At right is a large door, much more than man-size. It has a look of complicated and manifold function, and seems as if it might be organic, for it is hard to see how the thing is fastened into the rock. There is no jamb, lintel or frame. It seems more as if all that part of the rocky wall is, simply, door. And while it might be of brass, or bronze, or perhaps gold — any metal that by age comes to soften and glisten so that it coaxes and beguiles the eye — it might equally be made of some modern substance, glass, or plastic, or sound waves made visible. A faint humming sound can be heard, but it is more reasonable to assume that such a noise must come from the machines, even though these look dead — just as the eye is first drawn to them, in their central position, and not immediately to the great door, perhaps just because of its size and equivocal substance. Yet, once seen, the great door dominates, although, in contrast to the altar of technical objects, it looks neglected or ignored. The steps leading to it are undecorated.*

*At right front is a large round table with chairs set round it, glasses of water, scribbling blocks — the paraphernalia of a modern conference.*

*One is in progress. On the breast of each* DELEGATE *is a large badge with his or her status on it. They have no names. Each wears some sort of uniform, or stiff, formal clothing. The* DOCTOR *is dressed like a surgeon in an operating theatre. The* GUARDIAN OF THE DOOR *wears overalls like a mechanic, but he has religious and national symbols pinned or draped on him.*

*There are* ATTENDANTS *at the exit, left, and* GUARDS *behind the chairs of the* CHAIRMAN *and the* GUARDIAN OF THE DOOR.

CHAIRMAN: And that brings us to the end of our agenda. Thank you, all officers. Thank you, delegates.

*[People are already beginning to get up, but]*

FIFTH PRECEPT: Excuse me, not quite the end.

*[*CHAIRMAN *leafs to the end of his agenda, looks enquiringly at* FIFTH PRECEPT, *then laughs. So do some of the other.]*

FIFTH PRECEPT: I wasn't joking, sir.

*[They sit down again, but they still smile as if at an old joke.]*

CHAIRMAN: Fifth Precept, we have been in continuous session for nearly a week.
FOURTH PRECEPT: Or for several hundred years.
CHAIRMAN: Quite, quite. Fourth Precept, I do not think this is the right time for . . . it makes me nervous when anyone even jokes about time, measurements of time − that sort of thing, when it takes so little to start the bickering and disagreement off again. All very sincere people, very sincere, the historians and time-keepers, but . . .
FOURTH PRECEPT: I wasn't joking either, sir.
FIFTH PRECEPT: We would like to have the last item, Item 99, discussed and voted on.
FOURTH PRECEPT: Yes.
CHAIRMAN: When was the last time Item 99 was discussed, Secretary?
SECRETARY *[leafing through minutes]*: Just a moment. It's been so long that . . .
CHAIRMAN: Oh never mind.

FIFTH PRECEPT: It was fifteen years ago.

SECRETARY: Yes. That's right.

FIFTH PRECEPT: Which was when the problem arose last time.

GUARDIAN OF THE DOOR: There was a great deal of trouble. We had a lot of trouble, I remember.

CHAIRMAN: So I submit it can wait until tomorrow.

GUARDIAN: Or even next week.

[*The* DELEGATES *laugh.*]

FIFTH PRECEPT: No. It must be now.

CHAIRMAN: Forgive me, Fifth Precept, but are you feeling well? We are all of us pretty tired, and it is quite understandable . . .

FIFTH PRECEPT: Quite well, thank you. [*he stands up*] Exalted Chairman! Guardian of the Door! Fellow Precepts! Delegates! Secretaries! . . . and so on and so on and so on. If you actually take the trouble to look at the wording of the last item, Item 99 [*Some members hurriedly do so.*], You'll see that it reads: 'In view of the urgency, it is decided that full mobilization is called at once. The Door is expected to open at hour zero.' Very shortly, in fact. [*There is general discreet amusement.*] A great many people are expecting it.

CHAIRMAN: You know quite well that some nut is always announcing the Opening of that Door.

SECRETARY: Which is why we have Item 99 permanently on the Agenda, to take care of it.

FIFTH PRECEPT: Yet we all believe that the Door will open some time. And that when it does we can leave this place.

DELEGATE: Of course we do.

DELEGATE: Of course.

CHAIRMAN: If there had been any indication from Centre [*he indicates the machines and their worshippers*] we would have been told.

FIFTH PRECEPT: Our life in this place is entirely organized around our expectation of this Opening. If we didn't believe that we would one day escape, that our people would one day reach the open air and the light-of-day . . .

DELEGATE: Whatever they may be!

FIFTH PRECEPT: . . . the light-of-day, it would not be possible to sustain life here.

DELEGATE: Hear, hear.

SECRETARY: Article 17 of our Declaration of Faith. Very fine, but is a conference the right place for this sort of thing?

GUARDIAN: As First Guardian of the Door I must protest against the tone of our Secretary.

SECRETARY: Sorry, Guardian. [as GUARDIAN *does not relent, he recites*] I offer my thoughts, being and intentions in total apology for blasphemy. Unintentional blasphemy atonable for by simple-form apology.

GUARDIAN: Simple-form apology accepted with warning.

CHAIRMAN: Can we get on? I adjourn the conference until tomorrow.

FIFTH PRECEPT: I object.

CHAIRMAN: Overruled.

FIFTH PRECEPT: According to Rule 954 I have the right to insist.

CHAIRMAN: Wait a minute. [*he and* SECRETARY *consult the rules*] I see. Very well then – you're ill. You must be. I've never been more upset to see a colleague of mine fall under the weight of duty. You'd better take leave. From this evening.

FOURTH PRECEPT: And must I join him?

CHAIRMAN: Oh no, it's too much . . . when two of this, the highest body of our people, fall victim to . . . yes, both of you, take a month's leave.

A DELEGATE WHO HAS NOT YET SPOKEN: And me too?

[FOURTH AND FIFTH PRECEPTS *look at him in surprise, then at each other.*]

ANOTHER DELEGATE: And me?

[FOURTH AND FIFTH PRECEPTS *and the last speaker are surprised.*]

CHAIRMAN: Four of you. I see. I don't know why I didn't see it before – this is obviously yet another attempt from the Low-Levellers to take over. Obviously.

[FOURTH AND FIFTH PRECEPTS *and their two supporters laugh.*]

FIFTH PRECEPT: As soon as the Low-Levellers come into it, that's the end of all reason.

CHAIRMAN: We all know that you represent the Low-Levellers, that you work for their interests, that you improve their conditions – and of course, we all honour you for it.

FIFTH PRECEPT: Really? I hadn't noticed it.

CHAIRMAN: Of course, without reformers there's no progress. But. The Low-Levellers always overstep the mark sooner or later. We know that too, and expect it.

FOURTH PRECEPT: And make provision for it by putting under the last item of every agenda their requests, reasonable or otherwise, about the Door.

CHAIRMAN: I am glad you can admit they are sometimes unreasonable.

FIFTH PRECEPT: I and Fourth Precept assure you that this has nothing to do with the Low-Levellers.

THE TWO DELEGATES WHO SUPPORT THEM: Nothing. Nothing at all.

A DELEGATE: May we then ask who inspired your conviction that the Door is about to open?

FIFTH PRECEPT: For one thing, look at it.

[*They turn to look at the door in the middle of the stack of machinery.*]

CHAIRMAN: Well?

A DELEGATE: It has never changed since I first saw it.

ANOTHER: My father served on this committee and he said it never altered in his lifetime.

FIFTH PRECEPT: Not that Door. The other one.

A DELEGATE: What Door?

ANOTHER: What other Door?

CHAIRMAN: As you two are new on this committee, you may not know that certain deviant and of course unimportant sects have always maintained that the real Door is that one. [*He nods at the Door, right. The* GUARDIAN *coughs.*] I apologize.

GUARDIAN: It is not your fault these heresies continue.

DELEGATE: Funny, I never even noticed it.

GUARDIAN: Which is not surprising.

FOURTH PRECEPT: It is easily overlooked.

FIFTH PRECEPT: Until you have seen it – but then some people find it hard to look at anything else.

ONE WHO STARES AT THE ALTAR: Why, it isn't even attached to anything. It doesn't lead anywhere.

ANOTHER: It isn't anything at all.

GUARDIAN [*on his feet and obviously about to launch into an oration*]: My children, in this unfortunate time, let us all take heart and . . .

CHAIRMAN: Quite so, oh quite so, Guardian, but perhaps I should deal with this? [GUARDIAN *seats himself again*] Secretary, have you file Number 7? [SECRETARY *hands over file 7*] Last week, our investigators found evidence of a new subversive cult and . . .

FIFTH PRECEPT: You mean, our spies.

CHAIRMAN: If you like. But there is unrest. Serious unrest.

[*There is noise beyond the left opening. One of the* ATTENDANTS *comes running to the conference table.*]

ATTENDANT: Some of them insist on coming in.

CHAIRMAN: You have forgotten something, I think?

ATTENDANT: Second Hereditary Attendant to the Gate to the First Level. Some of them insist on coming in.

CHAIRMAN: They can wait until tomorrow.

[*A second* ATTENDANT *runs over.*]

THIS ATTENDANT: First Hereditary Attendant. They've got hand-grenades.

CHAIRMAN: I knew it. [*to a* GUARD] Arrest the Fourth and Fifth Precepts.

FIFTH PRECEPT: You haven't the authority.

CHAIRMAN: Haven't I!

SECRETARY: Precepts cannot be arrested without a week's full notice and then only after having posted . . .

CHAIRMAN: Oh never mind. Doctor – Precept Doctor?

[DOCTOR stands up]

FIFTH PRECEPT: There's no appeal against that.
CHAIRMAN: No.

[*The* DOCTOR *takes* FOURTH *and* FIFTH PRECEPTS *over to right. He claps his hands. Two white-overalled* MEDICAL ASSISTANTS *come running from left with a rolled stretcher, bottles of pills, a syringe. All the* DELEGATES *are watching these arrangements. The two who supported* FOURTH *and* FIFTH PRECEPTS *rise and go over and join them.*]

SECRETARY: Heroic!
CHAIRMAN: But futile.
FIRST HEREDITARY ATTENDANT: Exalted Chairman, they give us five minutes. They have the pins out of their grenades.
CHAIRMAN: We bow to force. Let them in.

[*Two* LOW-LEVELLERS *come in. They are dressed in sweaters and jeans, have long hair, carry grenades.*]

CHAIRMAN: Who are you?
FIRST LOW-LEVELLER: That doesn't matter.
CHAIRMAN: We must know with whom we are dealing.
SECOND LOW-LEVELLER: We are from Level 56.

[*Murmurs of shock and surprise from the* DELEGATES.]

FIRST LOW-LEVELLER: Yes, this is the first time any one of you have set eyes on Level 56-ers, isn't it?
CHAIRMAN: Your status?
SECOND LOW-LEVELLER: Oh tell them, if it keeps them happy.
FIRST LOW-LEVELLER: Officer First Class, Second Subsidiary Grade.
SECOND LOW-LEVELLER: Officer First Class, Second Subsidiary Grade.
FIRST LOW-LEVELLER: *Elected* officers.
CHAIRMAN: Impossible.
SECRETARY: Sir, there was that revolution last month in the Intermediate City.

CHAIRMAN [*affable*]: Ah, so you are the leaders of the successful coup in the Intermediate City?

FIRST LOW-LEVELLER: You can put it like that if you can't, understand it any other way.

[*From the left comes a muffled shout.*]

We have no leaders!

[*Some more* LOW-LEVELLERS *come into view, trying to force their way past the* ATTENDANTS. FIRST *and* SECOND LOW-LEVELLERS *turn so that they are able simultaneously to keep the* DELEGATES *controlled with their hand-grenades, and watch the entrance left.* THIRD *and* FOURTH LOW-LEVELLERS *burst in, with rifles. They are wearing a lot of leather, and have short hair.*]

THIRD LOW-LEVELLER: It is no use trying to keep us out.

CHAIRMAN: Very well, I suppose there is nothing for it. I declare the conference reopened, for discussion on Item 99. Will you please all be seated?

FOURTH LOW-LEVELLER: A committee! Would you believe it!

FIRST LOW-LEVELLER: We might have known it.

SECOND LOW-LEVELLER: I'm not wasting my time talking.

THIRD LOW-LEVELLER: I'll give you exactly three minutes.

FOURTH LOW-LEVELLER: And don't imagine we wouldn't use them.

CHAIRMAN: You don't want to discuss Item 99?

FIRST LOW-LEVELLER: We don't want to *discuss* anything.

GUARDIAN: What do you want then?

SECOND LOW-LEVELLER: To have full representation in the celebrations tomorrow.

THIRD LOW-LEVELLER: The Ceremony of the Garlanding of the Door.

CHAIRMAN: I'd almost forgotten about that. We have a rehearsal in a few minutes, haven't we?

GUARDIAN: Do you mind repeating that? You have forced your way in here because you want representation for Level 56 in the Garlanding Ceremony?

THIRD LOW LEVELLER: Not only so. All the levels beyond that too.

CHAIRMAN: But it's not physically possible to have representatives from all the hundred levels. That was why it was arranged by the First Ones that the levels from 1 to 50 should represent 50 to 100.

GUARDIAN: But after all, we haven't been faced with fifty extra people, only four.

FOURTH LOW-LEVELLER: It was never anything but a disgustingly unfair arrangement.

CHAIRMAN: Yet I see that you and your friend are happy to represent all the levels beyond 56. Isn't that so?

FIFTH PRECEPT: Exalted Chairman, may I remind you that we are placed here because you decided that we were part of this – demand?

A DELEGATE: Conspiracy!

ANOTHER DELEGATE: Undemocratic and violent overthrow of Constitutional Government!

CHAIRMAN: Well well, I don't know. Perhaps we of the upper levels have got a bit stuffy. I see no reason at all why Level 56 shouldn't be represented at the ceremony. And they may start by joining us in the rehearsal.

FIFTH PRECEPT: Just a minute. We were arrested because you believed us to be party to this demand, or conspiracy.

CHAIRMAN: You haven't been arrested.

FIFTH PRECEPT: Thank you.

[*He and the other three attempt to leave the group of* DOCTOR *and* MEDICAL ATTENDANTS, *but they are forcibly restrained*.]

FOURTH PRECEPT: We are being wrongfully held. On two counts. One, we knew nothing about this conspiracy. Two, it is now apparently not considered a conspiracy.

CHAIRMAN: Precept Doctor, we have not yet had your report.

FOURTH PRECEPT: There is no need of any report. We are all perfectly well.

DOCTOR: Of course this is only a provisional diagnosis, but in my opinion these patients are not fit to leave medical care.

FIFTH PRECEPT: We aren't patients.

DOCTOR: There. Come now. Relax. Take these pills. You are getting over-excited.

[*The two* PRECEPTS, *then the other two refuse the pills, as the* DOCTOR *threatens force.*]

FIRST LOW-LEVELLER: What's wrong with them? Who are they?

CHAIRMAN: You mean you don't even know your champions? Those are the famous Fighting Precepts.

FIRST LOW-LEVELLER: Champions!

SECOND LOW-LEVELLER: I think I've seen their pictures.

THIRD LOW-LEVELLER: Liberals!

FOURTH LOW-LEVELLER: Vacillating temporizers!

FIRST LOW-LEVELLER: Compromising timeservers!

CHAIRMAN: Well, well. And these are the people you have been fighting for.

FIRST LOW-LEVELLER: But what's wrong with them?

FIFTH PRECEPT: We are under medical care because we insist on discussing Item 99. Tonight.

SECOND LOW-LEVELLER: Never heard of it.

FIFTH PRECEPT: The Door is going to open. It is going to open.

THIRD LOW-LEVELLER: Oh I see, they're nuts.

GUARDIAN: I do so hope that you young people are not unbelievers. For while I deprecate the emotional extravagance and wrongheadedness of officers like the Fourth and Fifth Precepts, I find it in my heart to prefer that to total nullity.

FIFTH PRECEPT: But it is going to open.

FIRST LOW-LEVELLER: Well, of course it is. Who said it wasn't?

SECOND LOW-LEVELLER: We've all been taught that in school.

THIRD LOW-LEVELLER: Whether we liked it or not.

FOURTH LOW-LEVELLER: I didn't mind the Door lessons. I love those old myths.

GUARDIAN: Myths, indeed! Then why do you want to take part in the Door Ceremony?

FOURTH LOW-LEVELLER: It is a question of political equity.

FIRST LOW-LEVELLER: Justice.
SECOND LOW-LEVELLER: Liberty.
THIRD LOW-LEVELLER: Freedom.
FIFTH PRECEPT: But it will open. The Door will open. [*shouting*] Let me go. I must be free to tell everybody. I must . . .

[*The* MEDICAL ATTENDANTS *grab him. The* DOCTOR *deftly injects him, an* ATTENDANT *crams pills into his mouth. He passes out, and is laid on the stretcher. The* DOCTOR *tries to inject the* FOURTH PRECEPT, *who mimes submission, contrition, humility. As this is seen to work, the* DOCTOR *becoming avuncular and bland, the other two copy the* FOURTH PRECEPT. *Meanwhile* FOURTH PRECEPT *goes forward a little way to examine the big Door. He is joined by the two who have now mollified the* DOCTOR. *Do we imagine it, or is this Door brighter than it was?*]

THIRD LOW-LEVELLER: There have been a lot of pretty funny rumours down in the Levels recently.
CHAIRMAN: I would hardly describe a revolution as a rumour.
FIRST LOW-LEVELLER: No, about the Door. Rumours about the Door.
SECOND LOW-LEVELLER: More than rumours. There's a new sect.
THIRD LOW-LEVELLER: The main one calls itself 'The Door Will Open Soon' Society.
GUARDIAN: Indeed?
SECOND LOW-LEVELLER: There's been some rioting.
GUARDIAN: Very true. I had them arrested and imprisoned.
THIRD LOW-LEVELLER: I heard some escaped. We thought they might be here.

[FIRST *and* SECOND LOW-LEVELLERS *look suspiciously at* THIRD *and* FOURTH LOW-LEVELLERS, *while moving closer together.* THIRD *and* FOURTH *do the same. At the same moment, the two couples aim their grenades and their rifles at each other.*]

CHAIRMAN: Now, now. There's no need for that.

[*A fresh commotion outside left exit.* ATTENDANT *comes running over.*]

ATTENDANT: Second Hereditary Attendant of the Gate to the . . .

CHAIRMAN: Yes, yes, yes, yes, yes.

ATTENDANT: There's another lot.

CHAIRMAN: Then let them in, by all means.

[*This time there is a group of varying ages, and variously dressed. They are unarmed, and they walk quietly.*]

CHAIRMAN: Delighted to see you all.

GUARDIAN: Do come in.

SECRETARY: You are more than welcome.

DELEGATES: Hear, hear. Yes. Of course. Welcome.

ONE OF THE GROUP: Oh, I'm so glad. We thought we might not believe it.

CHAIRMAN: No, no, we think every Level should be represented. Every one, mark you, including Levels 50 to 100. You will all be welcome at the Ceremony. And indeed, we were just about to start the rehearsal for tomorrow.

GUARDIAN: And it is time to start. Do join us.

[*He stands facing the pile of machinery, as if heading a procession. The* DELEGATES *and officers start forming behind him.*]

ONE OF THE GROUP: But why does there have to be a Ceremony? Aren't we just going to walk right out?

[*This person, then others of the group, look at the Door propped up on the altar, look at each other, shake their heads, then start looking around. One sees the big Door right, indicates it to the others. This group moves over towards it.*]

CHAIRMAN: Doctor, you have some more patients.

FOURTH PRECEPT: I'm glad you made it. But be quiet. Don't argue. Don't fight.

[*This new group, the* FOURTH PRECEPT, *his two allies, are now close to the big Door. It is hard now to doubt that it is brighter. And surely the humming sound is louder.*]

FIRST LOW-LEVELLER: I've never seen any of that lot before.

THIRD LOW-LEVELLER: I wonder what Level they are from?

ONE OF THE NEW GROUP: We come from all the Levels. Not just from one.

FOURTH LOW-LEVELLER: Are you from 'The Door Will Open Soon' Society?

ANOTHER OF THE NEW GROUP: From all the societies.

ANOTHER: Or from none.

GUARDIAN: Shouldn't we be getting on? Chairman?

CHAIRMAN: Of course. Assistant to the Guardian of the Door . . .

[*One of the* DELEGATES *whose function this is starts shepherding members of the Conference, and the* LOW-LEVELLERS, *into a neater line behind the* GUARDIAN. *He hands them garlands of plastic and paper flower.*]

GUARDIAN: I'll just run through my opening lines. [*as if delivering a sermon, but rather fast*] Many thousands of years ago, no one knows how many, a natural disaster or a war sealed us in this Under Place. We understand from the old records that a few survivors, known to us as The First People, laid the basis of this our society, excavating the First Level of the Under City. Water supplies were discovered and ensured, and the cultivation of mushrooms, our staple food, begun. The Sacred Machines were placed here, at the gate of the Outside, for it was revealed to the First People that it will be the Sacred Machines which will announce to the Door the moment it must open . . . Etcetera and so on.

A DELEGATE: Lovely old stuff, isn't it?

ANOTHER: I've done this so often I could do it in my sleep.

ANOTHER: If the Door did actually open some of us would get the shock of our lives.

ANOTHER: We take it for granted there *is* something outside.

ANOTHER: Speak for yourself. I, for my part, am quite sure there is not.

ANOTHER: My attitude is that since we don't know, we should keep an open mind.

ANOTHER: Then why are you in this Ceremony at all? It is just hypocrisy.

CHAIRMAN: Nonsense, it is part of our ethic. Part of the fabric of our society.

DELEGATE: It does no harm and it may do some good.

SECRETARY: Refusing to take part in the Ceremony creates a disturbance. It is anti-social. It just draws attention to yourself, that's all.

GUARDIAN: Your reasons for being here are not important. There are many paths to the Door. [*to his* ASSISTANT] The regalia?

ASSISTANT: Here. [*He hands* GUARDIAN *the regalia, and assists him — a plastic smock with silver lightning flashes, a mitre, a small transistor radio in one hand, a telephone in the other. The latter is a child's toy, in a bright colour.*]

GUARDIAN: I think that's all. Assistant?

ASSISTANT: Lights. Lights. Turn down the lights.

[A TECHNICIAN *vainly clicks switches on the side of the computer.*]

TECHNICIAN: Sorry, but they don't seem to work. I've turned off the usual number of lights but it is no darker.

FOURTH PRECEPT: Look at the Door.

A MEDICAL ATTENDANT: It's much brighter.

DOCTOR: It's an optical illusion.

[*But now there is no doubt that the Door is brighter.*]

ONE OF THE NEW GROUP: It's getting brighter all the time.

GUARDIAN: Well, never mind. I'm sure the technicians will get everything right in time.

ANOTHER OF THE NEW GROUP: 'Wait and watch for the sudden time,
The song that's bright,
The singing light.'

[ASSISTANT TO THE GUARDIAN *tries to push* FIRST *and* SECOND LOW-LEVELLERS *to the back of the procession. They resist. He tries with the* THIRD *and* FOURTH LOW-LEVELLERS.]

FIRST LOW-LEVELLER: You don't seem to have got the point. Those days are over.

ASSISTANT: Everyone has to go where he is allocated.

FOURTH LOW-LEVELLER: No. Take your hands off.

CHAIRMAN: Move up here, behind me. We have got the point, I assure you.

[ASSISTANT *pushes* FIRST *and* SECOND LOW-LEVELLERS *up to the head of the procession behind* GUARDIAN.]

THIRD LOW-LEVELLER: Very nice.

ASSISTANT: You can't all four be up at the front.

GUARDIAN: Of course they can. The youth are our most precious possession, the gold of our future. Let them come.

[ASSISTANT *pushes* THIRD *and* FOURTH *into the procession behind* FIRST *and* SECOND LOW-LEVELLERS.]

THIRD LOW-LEVELLER: I'm sorry, but our status is just as relevant as their status.

FOURTH LOW-LEVELLER: It's not fair to those we represent.

ASSISTANT [*to* FIRST *and* SECOND LOW-LEVELLERS]: I am sure you are much too mature to mind. [*He pushes* THIRD *and* FOURTH *in front of them.*]

FIRST LOW-LEVELLER: No, I'm sorry. That won't do.

SECOND LOW-LEVELLER: It's the principle of the thing.

A DELEGATE: What is that noise?

[*All now look at the big Door, now glowing brilliantly. But is it responsible for that soft deep note?*]

THE SAME DELEGATE: Remember the old saying:
'When the Door begins to sing,
That's a sign of coming spring.'

GUARDIAN: We all know these old tales. But remember, there is no agreement about their origin.

ONE OF THE NEW GROUP: The First People left them for us as a signpost.

A DELEGATE: No. My father, and he was an expert in the field, said they were anonymous. They come spontaneously from the populace.

A DELEGATE: What is spring?

ANOTHER: They say that Outside it is beautiful in spring.

ANOTHER: What is beautiful? We all use the word, but what does it mean?

ANOTHER: Anything gets called beautiful.

ANOTHER: It was flowers and leaves. [*holding up some paper flowers*] Like this.

GUARDIAN: We have flowers and leaves.

THE DELEGATE WITH THE FATHER: My father said spring was a metaphor.

ANOTHER: My grandfather who was an expert said that flowers and leaves Outside are not like this, they are made of flesh.

THE DELEGATES, VARIOUSLY: Oh how disgusting. Revolting. Horrible. Repulsive. Ugh!

DELEGATE WITH THE GRANDFATHER: My grandfather had the theory that the word spring meant when Outside was covered all over with live tissue in different colours. You know, like our flesh, but different.

A DELEGATE [*shuddering*]: Like a sort of cancer.

DELEGATE: That would take a lot of getting used to for a start.

ANOTHER: That's what I've always said. I mean, we take it for granted that Outside would be better than here. But, ugh, flowers and leaves made of flesh, living flowers and leaves, I mean to say. [*He looks as if he is going to be sick.*]

FIRST LOW-LEVELLER: My father spent all his life studying the old sayings. His version of the spring verse is quite different.

SECRETARY: You have scholarship down on the Lower Levels? Yes, yes of course you do ...

[SECRETARY *exchanges a tolerant grimace with the* CHAIRMAN.]

FIRST LOW-LEVELLER: He said it should go:
'The Door will sing,
Then through it spring.'

THIRD LOW-LEVELLER: I like the other one better.

FIRST LOW-LEVELLER: Here, you two can't stay there. You can't be in front of us. I don't care for myself but it is an insult to the 56th Level.

FOURTH LOW-LEVELLER: We aren't moving back and that's final.

CHAIRMAN: I do hope you will forgive me intruding, but I

have a suggestion. You can't have been Hereditary Exalted Chairman all your life without learning something of the arts of compromise. [*He whispers to* ASSISTANT.]

ASSISTANT: You move there ... [*He pushes* FIRST LOW-LEVELLER *with* FOURTH.] ... and you there ... [*He pushes* THIRD *with* SECOND.]

[*There is violent scuffling and disorder.*]

FIRST LOW-LEVELLER: I'm not going to be with him. Look at his hair, if there wasn't anything else wrong.

THIRD LOW-LEVELLER: He makes me sick.

THE DELEGATE WHO COMPLAINED OF THE NOISE BEFORE: I'm sorry but I can't stand it. I have always been sensitive to noise. [*This one runs out, left, hands clapped to ears.*]

[*The Door, glowing brilliantly, is sending out a strong sweet sound.*]

FOURTH PRECEPT: 'The Door will sing.'

ONE OF THIS GROUP: 'The Door is singing, chanting, ringing,
The Door is shining, burning clear,
Leave your prison, the time is here!'

DELEGATE WHOSE FATHER WAS AN EXPERT: That's not the right version. I'm sorry.

ANOTHER FROM THE GROUP: 'The Door will glow,
It's time to go.'

SAME DELEGATE: No, that's wrong.

ANOTHER: No, it isn't, I've heard that version often.

[*A babble of quarrelling breaks out in the procession. At the same time, all the group near the door, including the* DOCTOR *and* MEDICAL ATTENDANTS, *press closer to it. The* ATTENDANTS, *at a sign from* FOURTH PRECEPT, *pick up the stretcher with* FIFTH PRECEPT.]

GUARDIAN [*taking command of the procession*]: This is a procession of Peace. Peace, I tell you.

FIRST LOW-LEVELLER [*grabbing* SECOND LOW-LEVELLER *and pulling him beside himself*]: You belong here.

GUARDIAN: Arrest the Low-Levellers.

[GUARDS *come forward to arrest them, but the four* LOW-LEVELLERS *spring out of the procession and stand in a group facing the* GUARDS, *weapons at ready.*]

FIRST LOW-LEVELLER: We'll blow the whole place up.

FOURTH LOW-LEVELLER: And don't think we don't mean it.

DOCTOR: This must be a mass hallucination. It's hypnosis. It's a trick.

[*The Door is now a flood of brilliant light, while from it comes a beautiful deep note.*]

ONE OF THIS GROUP: 'The atoms dance,
   The Door's on fire,
   The electrons sing,
   Now seize your chance.'

ANOTHER: 'Watch and wait,
   Know the time,
   A singing Door,
   That's the sign.'

FOURTH PRECEPT: Come on. [*He signals the* MEDICAL ATTENDANTS *to the Door.*]

DOCTOR: Stop.

[*The* MEDICAL ATTENDANTS *stop with the stretcher at the Door. All this group press up close, almost touching the Door. The* DOCTOR *hangs back a little, but he is being drawn slowly forward.*]

GUARDIAN: In the name of the Door I command you to disarm.

FIRST LOW-LEVELLER: Silly old fools. Scared. Like a lot of sheep.

SECRETARY: Not sheep. Ship. Scared like a lot of ship. Ship, plural of sheep.

SECOND LOW-LEVELLER: What's a sheep anyway? What's it matter?

SECRETARY: It matters very much. We must preserve standards. When we do eventually leave this Underplace and go out again, into Outside, then we'll need to know these things.

FOURTH LOW-LEVELLER. We don't even know what the Door is for. It's just there.

[*He rushes over and kicks the Door on the altar.*]

THIRD LOW-LEVELLER: There, you see? Nothing happens. [*He kicks the Door too. Stands defying it.*] Go on, punish me then!
FOURTH PRECEPT: 'A singing Door,
That's the time . . .'

[*He walks into the blaze of the Door and disappears. The others of that group follow, the* MEDICAL ATTENDANTS *taking the stretcher through last.*]

DOCTOR: I must be mad!

[*He goes into the Door like the others. A couple of people rush across from the left, ignoring the procession, going straight to the Door.*]

THESE SHOUT: Are we too late?

[*They jump into the light and vanish.*]

FOURTH LOW-LEVELLER: Did you see that? Did you?

[*He rushes across and jumps into the light.* FIRST LOW-LEVELLER *does the same. One of the* GUARDS *goes after him. But are we imagining it, or is the light slightly less, the deep note a little higher and fainter?*]

GUARDIAN [*he has noticed nothing*]: As Guardian of the Door, I command you, finally, to submit to me.
CHAIRMAN: As Exalted Chairman I order you to give yourselves up.
GUARDIAN'S ASSISTANT: According to Regulation 37d you have no alternative but to disarm.
SECOND LOW-LEVELLER: Silly old ships.

[*He throws his grenade at the computer. It explodes in smoke and flying fragments. There is indiscriminate scuffling, shouting.*]

*The Door is now fading rapidly, and the sound is nearly back to
its normal low humming.*
*Order is being restored over by the altar.* SECOND *and* THIRD
LOW-LEVELLERS *are disarmed and under arrest. A delegate lies
dead.*]

CHAIRMAN: That's over. We didn't allow ourselves to be
intimidated.

GUARDIAN: I'm delighted to see that my authority still has
force. And now I must make a plea for clemency.

CHAIRMAN: Of course, they were misguided, that's all. And
perhaps we were not without faults ourselves. We are perhaps
too ignorant of what goes on in the Levels below 50.

DELEGATES: Hear, hear.

CHAIRMAN: I move that we appoint a commission to inves-
tigate ways and means to strengthen our ties with the levels
below 50.

ASSISTANT TO GUARDIAN: But where are the other two
Low-Levellers?

DELEGATE: When it came to the point, they got scared!

CHAIRMAN: Doctor, take these two young people into your
care, will you? I am sure you don't mind a couple of extra
patients ... Where is the Doctor? Where have they all
gone?

A DELEGATE: I saw them all run through the light. I mean,
through the Door. They ran through the singing ... I saw
them.

CHAIRMAN: You saw what?

THIS DELEGATE: I saw them. I saw what happened. They've
escaped! They've got out. They've left this Underplace for
Outside! [*He runs to the Door and beats his hands on it, trying
to press himself through.*] They are free, I tell you. Free, free,
free!

CHAIRMAN: Guard, take this poor man to the hospital ...
where's the other guard? Oh never mind. And the two Low-
Levellers as well.

[GUARD *takes this* DELEGATE, *and two* LOW-LEVELLERS *out
left.*]

**⋯⋯ ⋯⋯⋯⋯ ⋯⋯** But I did see it, I did. Oh why was I such a fool? Why did I forget? . . . [*he recites as he is pulled out of sight*]

> 'If you miss the place and time,
> The Door again will sing and shine.'

THE DELEGATE WITH THE FATHER: That's not how that goes. It should go like this:

> 'The song was sung,
> The moment's gone,
> Light and sound together came,
> Those who did not catch the time,
> Must watch until it comes again.'

THE DELEGATE WITH THE GRANDFATHER: That's not the way my grandfather knew it . . . He said it should go like . . .

CHAIRMAN: Another time, please. Is everyone ready now?

[*He takes his place beside the* GUARDIAN. *The* ASSISTANT TO THE GUARDIAN *hands them both garlands, hangs more around their necks. Some music starts up.*]

ASSISTANT: Lights down please.

[*The* TECHNICIANS *turn down the lights. The Door can be seen glowing faintly in the half dark.*]

CHAIRMAN: There you are, the technicians have got the lighting right – I said they would.

# EACH HIS OWN WILDERNESS

This play was first presented by The English Stage Society, at The Royal Court Theatre, London, on 23 March 1958, with the following cast:

| | |
|---|---|
| TONY BOLTON | Colin Jeavons |
| MYRA BOLTON | Valerie Taylor |
| SANDY BOLES | Philip Bond |
| MIKE FERRIS | Vernon Smythe |
| PHILIP DURRANT | Ewen MacDuff |
| ROSEMARY | Sarah Preston |
| MILLY BOLES | Patricia Burke |

Directed by John Dexter

The action takes place in the hall of Myra Bolton's house in London.

# CHARACTERS

MYRA BOLTON: A middle-aged woman.

TONY BOLTON: Her son, aged 22.

MILLY BOLES: A middle-aged woman, Myra's friend.

SANDY BOLES: Milly's son, aged 22.

MIKE FERRIS: An elderly Left Wing politician.

PHILIP DURRANT: A middle-aged architect.

ROSEMARY: A young girl engaged to Philip.

# Act One

## SCENE I

*Before the curtain rises, an H-bomb explosion.* CURTAIN UP *on the sound of blast. Silence. Machine-gun fire. The explosion again. These sounds come from a tape-recording machine which has been left running. This is the hall of* MYRA BOLTON'S *house in London, stairs ascending L back. Door L into living-room. Door R which is entrance from street. Window R looking into garden at front of the house.*

*The essential furniture is a divan close to the foot of the stairs. A cupboard in the wall. A mirror. Odd chairs. A small radio.*

*Everything is extremely untidy: there are files, piles of newspapers, including the* New Statesman, *posters lying about inscribed* BAN THE BOMB, WE WANT LIFE NOT DEATH, *etc. A typewriter on the floor. The radio is playing tea-room music behind the war-noises from the tape-recorder.*

*After the second explosion* TONY BOLTON *comes in R. He is in Army uniform and has this day finished his Army service. He is a dark, lightly built, rather graceful youth, attractive and aware of it, but uneasy and on the defensive in the same way and for the same reasons as an adolescent girl who makes herself attractive as a form of self-assertion but is afraid when the attention she draws is more than gently chivalrous. His concern for his appearance is also due to the longing for the forms of order common to people who have never known order. He is at bottom deeply uneasy, tense and anxious, fluctuating between the good manners of those who use manners as a defence, the abrupt rudeness of the very young, and a plaintive, almost querulous appeal.*

*He stands looking at the disorder in the room, first ironically and then with irritation. As the music reaches a climax of bathos, he rushes to the radio and turns it off.*

TONY: What a mess. God, what a mess!

[*The sound of an H-bomb explosion gathering strength on the tape recorder. He turns to stare, appalled. Listens. Switches it off at explosion. There is a sudden complete silence.* TONY *breathes it in. He passes his hands over his hair, his eyes. He opens his eyes. He is staring at the window. Sunlight streams across the floor. He dives at the window, draws the curtains, making a half-dark, goes to the divan, lets himself fall limp across it. A moment's complete silence. The telephone rings.*]

[*querulously*] Oh, no, no, no. [*leaps up, goes to telephone*] Yes. It's me, Tony. No, I'm not on leave. I don't know where my mother is. I haven't seen her yet. Yes, Philip. I'll tell her. Who did you say? Who's Rosemary? OK. [*lets receiver fall back and returns to the divan, where he lies as before, eyes closed*] [MYRA'S VOICE *upstairs, singing*: Boohoo, you've got me crying for you.]

MYRA'S VOICE: Where are you, darling? [*continues singing*].

[*She comes into sight at the head of the stairs. A good-looking woman of about 45 or 50, and at the moment looking her age. She is wearing bagged trousers and a sweat-shirt. She peers down into the half-lit hall from the top of the stairs, and slowly comes down.*]

TONY [*languidly*]: Well, Mother, how are you?

MYRA: Tony! You might have let me know. [*She rushes at the window, pulls back the curtains, turns to look at him, the sunlight behind her.*]

TONY [*shading his eyes*]: Do we have to have that glare?

MYRA: Have you got leave?

TONY [*without moving*]: I didn't imagine it was necessary to remind you of the date my National Service finished.

MYRA: Oh, I see.

TONY: But, of course, if my coming is in any way inconvenient to you, I'll go away again.

MYRA [*stares and then laughs*]: Oh, Tony . . . [*rushes across at him*] Come on, get up out of that sofa.

[*He does not move. Then he languidly rises. She impulsively embraces him. He allows himself to be embraced. Then he kisses her gracefully on the cheek.*]

MYRA  Ohh! What an iceberg! [laughs, holding him by the arms]
[Suddenly he convulsively embraces her and at once pulls away.]
Oh, darling, it is lovely to have you home. We must have
a party to celebrate.

TONY: Oh, no.

MYRA: What's the matter?

TONY: A party. I knew you'd say a party.

MYRA: Oh, very well. [examining him, suddenly irritated] For
God's sake get out of that ghastly uniform. It makes you
look like a . . .

TONY: What?

MYRA: A soldier.

TONY: I've been one for two years.

MYRA: Isn't that long enough?

TONY: I think I'm rather sorry to part with it. [teasing her, but
half-serious] Rather nice, the Army – being told what to do,
everything in its place, everything tidy . . .

MYRA: Tidy! It's lucky you weren't in Cyprus or Kenya or
Suez – keeping order. [laughing angrily] Keeping everything
tidy.

TONY: Well?

MYRA: You don't believe in it. [as he does not reply] You might
have been killed for something you don't even believe in.

TONY: You're so delightfully old-fashioned. Getting killed for
something you believe in is surely a bit of a luxury these
days? Something your generation enjoyed. Now one just –
gets killed. [He has intended this to sound calmly cynical, but in
spite of himself it comes out plaintive.]

MYRA [has an impulse to make a maternal protective gesture, suppresses
it at the last moment. Says quietly, but between her teeth]: All the
same, get out of those clothes.

TONY [angry, because he knows he has sounded like a child]: All
right – but what do you suppose you look like?

MYRA [cheerfully]: Oh, the char, I know. But I've been cleaning
the stairs. If I'd known you were coming . . .

TONY: Oh, I know, you'd have changed your trousers.

MYRA: I might even have worn a dress.

TONY [*languidly charming*]: Really, Mother, when you look so charming when you try, do you have to look like that?

MYRA [*cheerfully impatient*]: Oh, don't be such a little — no one can look charming cleaning the stairs.

TONY [*unpleasantly*]: So you were cleaning the stairs. And who did you expect to find sitting here?

MYRA: Why, no one.

TONY: You came creeping down. Were you going to put your hands over my eyes and say: 'Peekaboo'? [*gives a young, aggressive, unhappy laugh*]

MYRA: It was dark. I couldn't see who it was. It might have been anybody.

TONY: Of course, anybody. Why don't you put your hands over my eyes now and say 'Peekaboo'? How do you know? — I might rather like it. Then you could bite my ear, or something like that. [*gives the same laugh*]

MYRA [*quietly*]: Tony, you've just come home.

TONY: Well, and why did you come creeping down the stairs?

MYRA: I came down because the telephone was ringing earlier. I came to see. Did you take it?

TONY: So it was. Yes. I forgot.

MYRA [*cheerfully*]: You're a bloody bore, Tony.

TONY [*wincing*]: Do you have to swear?

MYRA: Well, now you're home I suppose I'll have to stop. [*in a refined voice*] There are times, dear, when you do rather irritate me.

TONY [*stiffly*]: I've already said that I'm quite prepared to go somewhere else if it's inconvenient for you to have me at such short notice. [MYRA *watches him: she is on the defensive.*] Well? Who is that you've got upstairs with you? Who is it this time?

MYRA: How do you know I've got anyone upstairs with me?

TONY: Who *is* it upstairs?

MYRA [*offhand*]: Sandy.

TONY: Sandy who?

MYRA: Don't be silly. Sandy Boles.

TONY [*staring*]: But he's my age.

MYRA: What of it?

TONY: He's my age. He's 22.

MYRA: I didn't ask to see his birth certificate when I engaged him.

TONY: Engaged him?

MYRA [briskly]: He's at a loose end. I wanted someone to help me. He's here for a while.

TONY [slowly]: He's staying here?

MYRA: Why not? This empty house . . . when you're not here it's so empty.

TONY: He's in my room?

MYRA: Yes. He can move out.

TONY: Thanks. [They stare at each other like enemies.]

MYRA: Well, what is it?

TONY: Perhaps you'd rather I moved out.

MYRA: Tony, mind your own bloody business. I've never interfered with anything you did.

TONY: No [half-bitter, half-sad]. No, you never did. You never had time.

MYRA [hurt]: That's unfair.

TONY: And where's dear Sandy's mamma?

MYRA: Milly is in Japan.

TONY: And what is dear Sandy's errant mamma doing in Japan?

MYRA: She's gone with a delegation of women.

TONY [laughing]: Oh I see. They are conveying the greetings of the British nation, with an apology because our Government uses their part of the world for H-bomb tests.

MYRA [wistfully]: Is it really so funny?

TONY [not laughing]: Hilarious. And why aren't you with them?

MYRA: Because I was expecting you.

TONY [plaintively]: But you'd forgotten I was coming.

MYRA [irritated]: I might have forgotten that you were expected home at four o'clock on Tuesday the 18th March, 1958, but I was expecting you. Otherwise, of course, I would have gone with Milly.

TONY: But Milly didn't deny herself the pleasure on Sandy's account. He could fend for himself.

MYRA: You talk as if . . . Sandy's 22. He's not a little boy who needs his mother to wipe his nose for him. He's a man.

TONY [*terribly hurt*]: That must be nice for you. I'm so glad.

MYRA [*between her teeth*]: My God, Tony. [*She moves angrily away.*]

TONY: Where are you going?

MYRA: I'm going to demonstrate about the hydrogen bomb outside Parliament with a lot of other women. [*as* TONY *laughs*] Yes, laugh, do.

TONY: Oh, I'm not laughing. I do really admire you, I suppose. But what use do you suppose it's going to be? What good is it?

MYRA [*who has responded to his tone like a little girl who has been praised*]: Oh, Tony, but of course it's some good. Surely you think so?

TONY: You've been demonstrating for good causes all your life. So many I've lost count. And I'm sure you have . . . And where are we now?

MYRA: How do you know things mightn't have been worse?

TONY: How could they possibly be worse? How could they?

[*He sounds so forlorn, almost tearful, that she impulsively comes to him where he sits on the arm of the sofa, and holds his head against her shoulder, laying her cheek against it.*]

One might almost think you were pleased to see me.

MYRA [*amazed*]: But of course I am. [*He smiles, rather sadly.*] Of course. [*gaily, moving away from him*] Tony, I must tell you about what I'm doing. You know we've got that big meeting the day after tomorrow.

TONY: Actually, not.

MYRA: We've advertised it in all the papers.

TONY: I never read newspapers.

MYRA: Oh. Well, it's tomorrow. And I've worked out a simply marvellous . . . wait, I'll show you. [*She is fiddling about near the tape-machine.*]

TONY: Do you have to? I thought you said you had to go to your demonstration?

MYRA: Yes, I must rush. I'll just do the end bit. It's a sort of symposium – you know, bits of idiotic speeches by politicians – like this . . . [*switches on machine*].

POMPOUS VOICE: People who object to the hydrogen bomb are simply neurotic!

MYRA: And this —

PULPIT VOICE: The hydrogen bomb must be regarded by true Christians as part of God's plan for humanity.

MYRA: And then war effects, you know.

TONY: War effects?

MYRA: Listen. [puts on machine]

[Medley of war noises. Then machine-gun fire. Then the beginning of a scream — a conventional bomb falling.]

TONY: For God's sake stop it.

MYRA [stopping machine]: What's the matter? You see, the thing is, people have no imagination. You've got to rub their noses in it. [starts machine again]

[The scream begins and gathers strength. TONY stands rigid, trembling. At the explosion he flings himself down on the divan, his arms over his ears.]

[taking needle off] There. Not bad, is it? [turning] Where are you? Oh, there you are. Don't you think it's a good idea?

[TONY sits limp on the divan, hand dangling, staring in front of him. He wipes sweat off his forehead slowly.]

I'm really very pleased with it. [She stands, looking out of the window, starts to hum.] I must go and get dressed and go out. I do wish you young people would join in these demonstrations. Why don't you? — we're such a middle-aged lot. Why do you leave it all to us? [hums] Well, I'll finish the work on the tape tonight.

TONY: I forgot to tell you, there was a telephone message. From Philip. He says he wants you to put up Rosemary. Tonight.

MYRA: Who's Rosemary?

TONY: Didn't you know? He's getting married. To Rosemary.

[MYRA slowly turns from the window. She looks as if she has been hit.]

MYRA: Philip is getting married?

TONY: So he said.

MYRA: And he wants *me* to put her up?

TONY [*looking at her curiously*]: Why not? You're old friends, aren't you?

MYRA: Old friends?

TONY: Well, aren't you?

MYRA [*laughing bitterly*]: Of course. Old friends. As you know.

TONY [*examining her, surprised*]: But you surely don't mind. It's been years since . . .

MYRA: Since he threw me over – quite.

TONY: Threw you over? You're getting very emotional all of a sudden, aren't you – all these old-fashioned attitudes at the drop of a hat – I was under the impression that you parted because your fundamental psychological drives were not complementary! [*with another look at her stricken face*] Threw you over! I've never seen you like this.

MYRA [*dry and bitter*]: If you've lain in a man's arms every night for five years and he's thrown you over as if you were a tart he'd picked up in Brighton for the week-end, then the word friend has to be used with – a certain amount of irony, let's say. [*briskly*] We've been good friends ever since, yes.

[TONY *slowly rises, stands facing her.*]

TONY: Why do you talk like that to *me*?

MYRA [*noticing him*]: What's the matter now? Oh, I see. [*contemptuous*] You're not five years old. Why do you expect me to treat you as if you were five years old?

TONY: Perhaps I am five years old. But this is after all an extraordinary outburst of emotion. Dear Uncle Philip has been in and out of this house for years. Whenever he's in London he might just as well be living here. I can't remember a time when you and Uncle Philip in animated conversation wasn't a permanent feature of the landscape.

MYRA [*drily*]: I am the woman Philip *talks* to, yes.

TONY: Why all this emotion, suddenly?

MYRA: He has not before asked me to put up his prospective wife.

TONY: For God's sake, why should you care? You've lain in

men's arms since, haven't you? Well, isn't that how you want
me to talk, like a big boy?

MYRA: I suppose you will grow up some day. [*goes to the foot
of the stairs*] When's she coming?

TONY: Some time later this evening, he said. And he's coming,
too. We're going to have a jolly family evening.

MYRA: You'll have to look after her until I get back. We must
be perfectly charming to her.

TONY: I don't see why you should be if you don't feel like it.

MYRA: You don't see why?

TONY: No. I'm really interested. Why?

MYRA: Pride.

TONY [*laughing*]: Pride! You! [*He collapses on the divan laughing.*]

MYRA [*hurt*]: Oh, go to hell, you *bloody* little . . .

[*Her tone cuts his laughter. He sits stiffly in the corner of the divan.
She makes an angry gesture and runs up the stairs. Before she is
out of sight she is humming: 'Boohoo, you've got me crying for
you'.* TONY *strips off his uniform and puts on black trousers and
a black sweater. He rolls up the uniform like dirty washing and
stuffs it into the knapsack. He throws the knapsack into a cupboard.
He stands unhappily smoothing back his hair with both hands.
Then he goes to the looking-glass and stands smoothing his hair
back and looking at his face. While he does this,* SANDY *very
quietly comes down the stairs behind him. He is an amiable young
man at ease in his world.*]

SANDY [*quietly*]: Hullo, Tony.

TONY [*still standing before the looking-glass. He stiffens, letting his
hands drop. He slowly turns, with a cold smile*]: Hullo, Sandy.

SANDY [*at ease*]: I see you've disposed of the war paint already.

TONY: Yes.

SANDY: That's a very elegant sweater.

TONY [*responding*]: Yes, it's rather nice, isn't it . . . [*Disliking
himself because he has responded, he stiffens up. He roughly rumples
up his hair and hitches his shoulders uncomfortably in the sweater.*]
Don't care what I wear.

SANDY: I'll move my things out of your room. Sorry, but we
didn't expect you today.

TONY: Next time we will give you good warning.

SANDY: Cigarette?

TONY: That's a very smart cigarette case. No thanks.

SANDY: Mother brought it back from China last year. You remember she went?

TONY: Yes, I remember. Mother went, too. I suppose one does have to go to China for one's cigarette cases.

SANDY: I'm rather fond of it myself. [*pause*] Did you know I was helping Myra with her work?

TONY: As a matter of interest, what work are you doing?

SANDY: Formally, secretarial. But in practice – your mother has every talent in the world but one.

TONY: A sense of timing?

SANDY: You wouldn't exactly call her tidy.

TONY: Perhaps that's the same thing.

SANDY: She does need someone to sort things out for her.

TONY: Luckily she realizes it. In fact she makes a point of having someone around for that purpose. [*As* SANDY *does not take this up* –] Do you remember James?

SANDY: James? The boy with the golden gloves? Of course. Actually your mother told me she had him here for a time last year when he was out of a job.

TONY: He wasn't actually living here. [SANDY *keeps his temper with an over-obvious effort.*] James is working for Shepherds now and doing very nicely, thank you. You know, the new publishers.

SANDY [*lightly*]: Your mother has been pulling strings for me, too. I'm starting in with Mike Ferris next week.

TONY: *What*? I didn't know your politics were Left Wing.

SANDY: As much Left as anything, I suppose. But these labels are all rather *vieux jeu*, aren't they?

TONY: Oh, quite so – that's just the phrase I was looking for. Well, perhaps she can fix me up in Mike Ferris's office, too. After all, I don't find the political labels just a little *vieux jeu*.

SANDY: I was under the impression you were going to finish studying for your degree.

TONY: You were? Why?

SANDY: I imagined ... well, I suppose I got the idea from Myra. I think she expects you to.

TONY: Really? I'm quite in the dark. Why should she?

SANDY: It was rather odd, your throwing it all up three weeks before the final exam. Training to be an architect is an expensive business, and then you threw it all up.

TONY: Mother said all that? She said all that to you? She's discussed it with *you*?

SANDY: No. But surely one is bound to think it? It's not everyone who can afford to spend four years studying and then throw it all up with three weeks to go.

TONY: Mother certainly couldn't afford it. And she quite rightly told me I would have to stand on my own feet from then on. Of course she didn't reproach me. One can scarcely imagine mother reproaching one for that sort of thing. Freedom of choice is everything. My mum is a great one for freedom. Odd, isn't it? [*He hums a bar or two of the* Internationale.] No, she merely said, in her inimitable way: 'Well, if you're determined to be illiterate, you'd better learn something useful. Like mending the electric lights.' So I took her at her word. I'm now a qualified electrician. Join the army and learn a trade.

SANDY [*whimsical again*]: I don't think she expects you to settle for being an electrician.

TONY: No? Why not? It was her suggestion. [*suspiciously*] What has she been saying to you?

SANDY: Nothing.

TONY: I expect she'll drop information about her plans for my future in her own good time. When she has a moment to spare from the H-bomb, perhaps.

[MYRA *appears at the head of the stairs. She looks beautiful, and one would hardly recognize her for the same woman. Her dress is elaborately smart.* TONY *looks at* SANDY, *winces as he sees his admiring face.* MYRA *descends, smiling with frank pleasure at the impression she is making.*]

TONY [*still looking at* SANDY]: We are repressing a desire to applaud.

MYRA: Oh, don't repress it. Please don't. [*reaching the foot of the stairs*] Where's my hat? [*rummaging about*] Where did I leave my hat?

TONY: What's your hat doing down here, anyway?

MYRA: Obviously I left it here when I took it off.

TONY: Why do you have to leave it in the hall?

SANDY: Darling, it's in the cupboard.

MYRA: Of course I did. [*She opens cupboard, seizes hat, throws out* TONY's *army things.*] You can't leave your battle-gear in here. It's my china cupboard.

TONY: Why do you have to keep your hat and your china in a junk cupboard in the hall? Oh, Lord, Mother!

[MYRA *puts on her hat in front of the looking-glass. It is a very smart hat.*]

SANDY: Darling, you look beautiful.

TONY: For God's sake, you aren't going to wear that for a demonstration outside the House of Commons? Why don't you chain yourself to the railings and be done with it?

MYRA: Why not? I've been telling the committee that it is gravely underrated as a political weapon. It is time it was revived.

TONY [*furious*]: Christ, and you would, too.

MYRA [*furious*]: Yes, and it would be so unladylike, wouldn't it? How the hell did I come to have such a tenth-rate little snob for a son . . . ? Oh, I'm sorry. Come on, give me a kiss.

[*She kisses him on the cheek. He suffers it.*]

I suppose you'll grow out of it. But if you only weren't so *glossy.*

TONY: Me, glossy!

MYRA [*in a fever of irritation*]: You're such a beautiful boy. [*to* SANDY, *half-laughing*] Isn't he a beautiful boy? [*almost growling*] Ohhh! Such a beautiful, glossy, well-groomed boy, and so neat in his habits.

TONY [*half-flattered, half-puzzled*]: Why are you so cross? You know quite well you look devastating and I'm bowled over. Do you want me to pay you compliments?

MYRA! Why not?

TONY: I thought that was what Sandy was here for.

[MYRA *and* TONY *glare at each other,* SANDY *turns away.*]

And now kiss Sandy too. On the cheek.

MYRA [*angrily*]: I was going to. Dear Sandy. [*She kisses* SANDY *soundly on both cheeks.*] And now I must run like the wind.

[*She makes a slow and impressive exit R, watched with affectionate admiration by* SANDY, *sardonically by* TONY.]

SANDY [*chuckling*]: Dear Myra. I've never known any woman with such a sense of gesture.

TONY [*coldly*]: Really? Gesture? She's sincere about this. She's sincere about war. It's no gesture.

SANDY [*chuckling*]: Of course she is. She's absolutely splendid. She's going to be at least an hour late. And she'll be ticked off by the committee again. Really so unjust, the work she puts into it. She was up till four this morning working out this tape-recording thing with me.

TONY: She was up till four? Really? [*gratefully*] You were both up till four.

SANDY: It's a magnificent job, it really is. Bits of speeches — she smuggled a tape recorder into the House. That took a bit of doing.

TONY: Illegal, of course.

SANDY: Oh, she's wonderful. Really wonderful propaganda. Asinine remarks from politicians, and war effects. She's worked in a terrific bit from Japan — you know, people dying as a result of the first atom bomb. And then children. That sort of thing.

TONY: Children.

SANDY: Children crying during a bombardment. Then machine guns and bomb noises. You really must hear it. [*going towards machine*] I'll put it on for you.

TONY [*violently*]: No.

SANDY: I think you'd be impressed. It's a splendid job.

TONY [*bitterly*]: I've no doubt it is. Splendid. [*goes to window*]

But I rather doubt whether she's going to get near enough to the House of Commons even to get ticked off for being late. Because she's in animated conversation with Uncle Mike in the middle of the street – she's just missed being run over. Dear Mother.

SANDY: And who's Uncle Mike?

TONY: Why, Mike Ferris – your prospective sponsor for your life as a fighter for the people.

SANDY: Why Uncle?

TONY: I've had so many uncles. Well, Uncle Sandy? Oh, don't bother to get out your boxing gloves so as to defend Mum's honour. You don't want Mike to find us brawling, do you? Besides, in these matters at least, I am a pacifist. [*looks out of window*] Dear Mike. The very image of a politician. The old type of politician – the platform rather than the committee man. [*back at* SANDY] And which are you settling for, Uncle Sandy? Of course, you're the committee man. One must keep up with the times, mustn't one? Sandy Boles, MP, backroom boy; Sandy Boles, centre of centre of the Labour Party. Yes, you're right, Sandy, it's the Labour Party for you – the road to ministerial position with the Tories is long and arduous and you haven't got the connexions. Oh yes, I can see you. Mr Sandy Boles, MP for Little Puddleditch, centre of centre. A sound man. Getting sounder and sounder as maturity sets in and you become certain that there are ever so many sides to every question . . .

SANDY [*extremely polite*]: Have a cigarette, Tony.

TONY: No thanks. He's coming in. [*He almost twists up with self-dislike.*] Why am I on to old Mike? I like him. I always have. He's the salt of the earth and all that. And I'm sure he's never said one thing and meant another in the whole of his life. Well, hardly ever. He'll never be Minister for anything. Not even an Under Secretary. Without people like him the whole show really would be a bloody circus. But he's so – bloody *innocent*. When he starts talking it makes me feel a thousand years old. Sometimes I think he's parodying the ordinary kind of political pomposity, and then, God help me, I see that he means every word. Every sweet silly word of it. Well . . .

suppose after all the simple-minded do gooders do turn up
trumps. We'd look silly then, wouldn't we – Mr Sandy Boles,
MP? Well, why shouldn't they? There's nothing left but
simple-minded honesty – and faith.

SANDY [*blandly interested*]: Faith in what?

TONY [*after a long pause, allowing himself to straighten up*]: I don't
know. Well? You can't possibly be prepared to go through
all the slot-machines? You can't be.

SANDY: What's the alternative?

TONY: Oh, *Christ*! Seven years or so of establishing oneself as
a *sound* young man. Marriage – for love, of course. Then
divorce. Perhaps several divorces. Who are we to think ourselves better than our parents? Oh well. You'll be all right,
Uncle Sandy. The glorious battle for socialism inside the
Labour Party will save you from all that, won't it? Oh, *Christ*!
Look at Mother's lot – fire-eating Socialists, every one of
them, and here they are, all sorted out into neat little boxes.

SANDY: As a matter of interest, what label would you stick on
the box Myra is in? Or my mother?

TONY [*after a pause, laughing*]: The dilettante daughters of the
revolution?

SANDY: Come, come. Dilettantes don't work.

TONY [*impatiently*]: Oh, they're women who haven't succeeded
in getting or staying married.

SANDY [*ronically*]: Well, well. Have a drink, Tony, do.

TONY: The only people I think I really admire are tramps.
Something like that. I hitch-hiked from camp. There were
two of us. The other chap was a man who threw up his job
ten years ago and he hasn't worked since. Earns enough to
keep eating. And drinking – he's a soak.

SANDY: *Sounds* all right.

TONY: We need a new form of – inner emigration. Drugs.
Drink. Anything. I want to opt out. I don't want any part
of it. [*at* SANDY'S *raised eyebrows*] Well, what are you suggesting? That I'll settle down?

SANDY: Of course.

TONY: I'm in a bad mood! You sound like mother. I'll get
over it, I suppose. Well, I suppose I will. All the same, what

I think now is the truth, not the lies I'll be telling myself in five years' time when I've put down the first deposit on my future. If there is a future.

SANDY: My dear chap, you really had better get drunk.

TONY: Drinking bores me. [*He throws away his cigarette.*] And smoking. [*and now he is a querulous child again*] And women.

SANDY [*blandly*]: Women too?

TONY: What on earth do you talk to them about? All they're interested in is – Oh, hell! You can't possibly sit there and tell me you really like women.

SANDY: But I adore women.

TONY: That's what I mean. [*irritated*] Oh, hell! – the truth is I don't care for anything in the world except this house.

SANDY: Are you going to take it on your back with you when you go tramping?

TONY: Look out, here's Mike.

[MIKE FERRIS *enters from R. He is a man between 55 and 60, portly, kindly, with the dignity that comes from sincerity and a sound conscience. There is no conflict between his public face and his private face: there never has been. He went into politics thirty years ago out of a simple and earnest conviction, and he has never lost his simplicity and his earnestness.*]

[*languidly good-mannered*] My dear Mike, how nice to see you.

MIKE: Well, Tony, old chap. How nice to see you back in civilized clothes.

TONY [*still like a Society hostess*]: Do sit down, Mike. Can I get you a drink?

MIKE [*smiling, a little amused*]: No thanks. I just popped in to say hullo. Your mother said you were back, and I said I'd pop in to have a look at you. It really is so good to have you home again.

TONY [*deflating suddenly into awkward sincerity*]: Sit down, Mike. Don't rush off. You must have a drink.

MIKE: It's very kind of you. Just for a minute then. [*to* SANDY] And we are all looking forward very much to having you in the office. You're joining us at an interesting time, you know.

SANDY [*gracefully*]: I'm looking forward to it, too.

MIKE: Though when you think of the big issue, the hydrogen bomb business, nothing else seems to matter so much, does it? [*accepting a glass from* TONY] The more I think about it, the more I am convinced it is much more simple than we think. Simply a question of getting the Governments to agree, that's all.

TONY [*drily*]: That's all?

MIKE: Well, it really is hard to believe that people will be prepared to do things that will affect their own children, isn't it? I really can't believe, when it comes to the point, that common sense won't prevail.

TONY: You really believe that the men in power care about other people getting hurt?

MIKE: My dear boy – well, no. After a lifetime in politics – no. But everything's so critical – obviously we can get agreement if we try.

TONY: Are you suggesting that the voice of the people will prevail? Or, to coin another phrase, that the people are on the march?

MIKE: If the voice of the people doesn't prevail, what will? I really can't believe – I *can't* believe that after all we've done, all the glorious achievements of humanity, we are going to consent to blowing it all up.

TONY [*puzzled, more than derisive*]: You can't?

SANDY [*very smoothly, as it were testing a public voice*]: Quite obviously, the first step is to stop tests everywhere, and then we can proceed to a general discussion on disarmament.

TONY [*staring at him with disgust*]: Oh, hear, hear!

MIKE: If the tests are stopped we still have the Lord knows how many hydrogen bombs stored here and there, waiting for some madman to set them off. But I can't believe humanity will be so stupid.

TONY [*with fierce sincerity*]: Why can't you believe it?

MIKE: But, my dear boy, we do seem to get through somehow. We get through the most appalling messes.

TONY [*fiercely*]: No, I really do want to know. Why can't you believe it? This is what interests me. Mother can't believe it either. Speaking for myself, I can believe it only too readily.

SANDY [*whimsically*]: Oh, I can't believe it.

MIKE: I'm so glad to hear that, Sandy. Because, generally speaking, you young people . . . well, well.

TONY: Why can't you and mother and the rest of you believe it? [*at* SANDY *derisively*] And *you*, of course, Sandy. [*to* MIKE] You seem to be constitutionally incapable of believing in the ultimate horrors. Why? You've lived through enough, haven't you? It gives me the creeps to listen to any of you when you're in one of your reminiscing moods — a record of murder and misery. Yet on you go, all jolly and optimistic that right will prevail.

MIKE [*with great sincerity*]: It's a question of getting agreement between men of good will everywhere.

TONY [*laughing incredulously*]: Good. Let's drink to that: the glorious achievements of humanity.

MIKE [*seriously*]: Yes. [*He lifts his glass to drink. Seeing* TONY'S *face, lowers it again.*] You're not looking too well, young Tony. And your mother's not looking too well either.

TONY: Mother's not looking well?

SANDY: Why, Myra's on top of her form.

MIKE: I thought she wasn't looking too well. [*wistfully*] She really does need someone to look after her.

TONY: I'm sorry you think I'm so inadequate.

MIKE: Yes. Well. But if you're going to start studying again —

TONY: But I'm not.

MIKE: You're not? What? But . . . I see. [*He is very disturbed.*] But, Tony, your mother . . . You do seem to have such a lot of problems, you young people. Of course one is rather bound to feel insecure with that Government we've got.

TONY: We can always look forward to the blissful security we'll have under the next Labour Government. [*as* MIKE *looks hurt*] There are also the American Government and the Russian Government. And how stand the Russians these days, Mike? In the right of it as usual?

MIKE: Tony, I do hope you're not getting at your mother over this business — she's feeling very bad about it, you know. A lot of people are. I am myself. It would be easy to say we

were wrong. But when it's a question of knowing you were
both right and wrong, and having to decide where you were
wrong — I wish you wouldn't get at Myra just now.

TONY [*irritated*]: Mike, I can't remember a time when the whole
lot of you weren't tortured by something happening thousands of miles away. I don't see that anything's changed
much.

MIKE: She's really so worried about everything.

TONY: Oh, I know she doesn't spare herself. But then she never
has.

MIKE: No, she never has. And she has had rather a tough time
of it. It's odd how some people's lives — well, well. I often
think of how your mother used to be when your father was
alive. They were so happy. I loved being with them. They
were such a happy couple. And then he was killed that night.

TONY: It is the night Mother refers to in her inimitable way
as the Night the Bomb Fell.

MIKE: Yes. And your father was killed and you and your mother
were buried alive for hours. [TONY *winces, turns away to hide
how much he is affected.*] Yes. Perhaps you could persuade your
mother to go away with you for a holiday somewhere.

TONY [*wistfully*]: With me? Mother? [*laughs*] With me?

MIKE: There's that cottage of mine in Essex. It's empty.

TONY: I shouldn't imagine that a cottage in Essex with me is
mother's idea of fun at all. [*at* SANDY] Do you fancy the
idea of a holiday in Essex, Uncle Sandy?

MIKE: Knowing that money is a bit short at the moment.

TONY: Yes, so I gather, but why?

MIKE [*evasively*]: Oh, one thing and another. For one thing she
gave up her job to do this hydrogen bomb work and of
course it's not paid. And . . . various things. I got the impression money was a bit short. And there's the cottage, empty.

TONY: It's very good of you. Thanks, Mike.

MIKE: The flat can wait. There's no problem about that.

TONY: The flat?

MIKE: I meant to tell Myra that it was all fixed up when I saw
her in the street, but it slipped my mind.

TONY: What flat?

MIKE: As it happened, when Myra asked me if I could help, I could. It's an ill wind that blows nobody any good. Joan – my daughter, you know – is leaving her husband. I don't know why. I thought it was a rather good marriage. But it's broken up. Very sad. Well, well. And there's the flat. Just right for *you*.

TONY: For me? A flat?

MIKE: Didn't you know? Myra seemed to think you'd be wanting a place of your own when you came out of the Army.

TONY: I see. [*looks at* SANDY] I see.

[*He walks out of the room, R, slamming the door.*]

MIKE: What's wrong?

SANDY: He'll get over it.

MIKE: Myra thought he'd prefer to be by himself. She's always been very anxious about being the possessive mother, you know. She said *she* had to fight to leave home, and she doesn't want Tony to feel he should stay at home just because she's lonely.

SANDY [*chuckling*]: Myra's lonely? But she's never alone.

MIKE: Yes, well. [*with deliberate pleasantness*] It must be nice to have you here.

SANDY [*whimsically*]: And nice for me.

MIKE: Yes, believe me, I'm glad. It's so nice to meet a young man who . . . there's my elder son. As far as I can make out he's a homosexual. Or if he's not, he might just as well be.

SANDY: I assure you, if it relieves your mind, that I'm not.

MIKE: Oh it does. And I'm pleased for both Myra and yourself that . . . not that I'm not jealous, I am.

SANDY: Mike, you really are wonderful.

MIKE: When I was young I had such a good time. I do believe that young people should have a good time. But they don't seem to. At least, none of my children seem to. They talk in the most sophisticated way, but when it comes to the point . . . And there's young Tony. Oh dear, he is in a mood. Well, that's one of the reasons Myra would like him to have his own flat. So he'd feel free. I think it would be better not to mention it again. So there's a perfectly good flat going begging.

SANDY: But he loves this house — or so he says. God knows why. It's such a mess. Besides, he *says* he wants to be a tramp.

MIKE [*seriously*]: He does, does he? Well, well. That's interesting.

SANDY: In order to escape the corruptions of modern life.

MIKE: Oh. I must tell Myra. She'll be delighted. Well, so I suppose you don't want a flat?

SANDY: I live at home with my mamma quite happily, thank you. I have the bottom half and she has the top half.

MIKE: That sounds reasonable. But you've never had the urge to leave home? To cast its dust off your feet?

SANDY: Good Lord, why should I? Besides, Mother's such a good cook. Almost as good as Myra.

MIKE: Don't you want to revolt against us? It was my first idea. And Myra's too. And she has been so looking forward to the moment when Tony would revolt against her.

SANDY: But how could one revolt against my mother or against Myra? They are both perfectly delightful. And besides, you've done all the revolting, haven't you? There's nothing left for us.

MIKE: Sure there must be something . . . a tramp. Good for him.

[TONY *comes in fast from R.*]

TONY: Mother and Philip are coming. Philip, but no Rosemary. [*to* MIKE] Do you know who Rosemary is?

MIKE: Rosemary? The only Rosemary I know is Rosemary Paine.

TONY: Who is Rosemary Paine?

MIKE: She used to be married to old Paddy — Secretary for — I forget now. She's interested in Housing. Yes. Nice woman. Very efficient.

TONY: Well, Philip is marrying her.

MIKE: Philip's marrying again, is he? Good for him.

TONY: We're in for such a jolly time. Mother, battling day and night — or at least, part of the night, with the Bomb. And Rosemary battling with Housing. And your mother, Sandy. Sandy, when's Milly coming back?

SANDY: Very soon now, I believe.

TONY: Milly will help mother to battle with the Bomb when she's not attending to racial prejudice and the Chinese peasantry. Oh, my God, they really are utterly intolerable. [*flinging himself down*] I simply cannot endure them. It's their utterly appalling vitality. They exhaust me.

SANDY: Perhaps it's time you took to the roads.

TONY: You don't seem to see the horrors of the situation. We're going to have this house full of Amazons. Three of them. My mother. Your mother, popping in and out with her hands full of pamphlets and files, as is her wont. And Rosemary.

[MYRA *and* PHILIP *come in R. They are laughing together, very gay and animated.* MYRA *is carrying her hat in her hand. As she enters she throws it on to a chair.* TONY *leaps up and bundles it into the cupboard.* PHILIP *is an attractive man of about 45.*]

MYRA: Did you say Rosemary? Has she come?

SANDY: No, she hasn't come yet; why aren't you outside the House of Commons, Myra?

TONY: Yes, why aren't you?

MYRA: Philip dropped in, we got talking, and I came back with him.

TONY: What do you mean, dropped in. You talk about the House of Commons as if it were the local.

PHILIP: I was driving past, and I saw Myra with the others, and I stopped to say hullo. Where's Rosemary? She said she'd get here under her own steam.

TONY: We are all sitting here waiting for Rosemary.

PHILIP: I do hope it's all right, her coming here.

MYRA [*gaily*]: Of course, where else should she come?

PHILIP [*a bit embarrassed*]: Well, I did try to fix her up somewhere else. Somewhere more central for shopping, I mean. [MYRA *smiles ironically at* PHILIP. *He responds unwillingly.*] Well, she says she can't get married without new clothes. [*turning away from* MYRA'S *irony*] Well, Mike – nice to see you again.

MIKE: Haven't seen you for some time, Philip. Haven't you
time for politics any longer?

PHILIP: I'm up to my eyes with this new community centre
we're building.

MIKE: Yes, I heard. So your firm got the contract? It's a big
thing, isn't it?

MYRA [delighted]: Philip, darling, why didn't you tell me. I'm
so glad.

PHILIP [turning to her – they instantly make a close, absorbed pair]:
Do you remember those plans I was playing with that summer
– when we were in Venice?

MYRA: But of course. They were beautiful. And you were in
despair because you said you'd never see it built. [MYRA and
PHILIP are close together under the window. MIKE, SANDY,
TONY stand separate, watching them.]

MIKE [trying to detach PHILIP from MYRA]: We've been missing
you on the committee, Philip.

PHILIP [who has not heard MIKE]: Myra, do you remember how
I wanted that façade – remember, you said it wouldn't work?

MYRA [laughing]: Then I was wrong. Remember how we quarrelled about it? We quarrelled for three days?

PHILIP [laughing]: What, we only quarrelled for three days that
time?

SANDY [jealous and loud, with a step forward]: I do so hope Rosemary is interested in architecture.

MYRA [who has not heard]: And what about the roof gardens –
did you get your way about those too?

PHILIP: Yes, everything. Look, I'll show you the photographs.

[PHILIP and MYRA stand side by side by the window, looking at
the photographs. The door R slowly opens; ROSEMARY stands
there. She is a girl of 19 or 20, a slight creature with a sad little
face. She wears black trousers and a black sweater. In general style
and type she is so similar to TONY she might very well be his
sister.

SANDY, MIKE, and TONY are watching the couple by the
window. No one notices her.]

MYRA: This is going to take up a lot of your time, Philip. I do hope you aren't going to drop out of politics altogether.

PHILIP: Myra darling, can't you see everyone's fed up with politics. It's not the time.

MYRA: What do you mean, not the time . . . ?

PHILIP: Not the old kind of politics. Surely you can see that? [ROSEMARY *takes a couple of steps forward.* TONY *sees her.*]

TONY [*to* ROSEMARY]: Can I do anything for you?

ROSEMARY: Well, yes.

TONY: My God, you aren't Rosemary?

ROSEMARY: Yes, I am. Who did you think I was?

TONY [*dramatically, to the* OTHERS]: Rosemary is here. [SANDY *and* MIKE *turn, are stunned into silence. Simultaneously* PHILIP *and* MYRA *raise their voices. They do nor hear* TONY *nor see* ROSEMARY.]

MYRA: Oh, Philip, for God's sake, you're not going to change, are you?

PHILIP: Well, why not?

MYRA: Philip, half the people I know, people who've spent all their lives fighting and trying to change things, they've gone inside their homes and shut their front doors and gone domestic and comfortable – and safe.

PHILIP: Well, what's wrong with that?

TONY [*shouting*]: Myra. Philip. Rosemary's here.

MYRA [*as she and* PHILIP *slowly turn*]: What's wrong with it? I never believed I'd hear you say that – who's that?

[PHILIP *sees* ROSEMARY, *drops his arm from* MYRA, *moves away from her.*]

ROSEMARY [*pathetically*]: Hullo, Philip.

**CURTAIN**

# SCENE 2

*It is next morning. The place is in total disorder. The divan has been slept in and is tangled all over with clothes, sheets, newspapers, pillows.* TONY *is lying flat on the floor. He is wearing his black trousers and a pyjama jacket.*

ROSEMARY, *dressed as she was yesterday, in black trousers and sweater, comes half-way down the stairs.* TONY *does not move.*

ROSEMARY: What are you doing here?

TONY: This house has eight rooms in it and this is the only corner I can find to fit myself into — together with mother's hat, the china and the rest of the . . . [*indicates the files, papers, etc.*]

ROSEMARY: What's in the other rooms?

TONY: People. And Things. More Things than People. Extraordinary how much space the humanitarian conscience takes up. [*He again indicates the paraphernalia in the hall.*]

ROSEMARY: I'm sorry we've taken your room.

TONY [*eagerly*]: It's a pretty room, isn't it?

ROSEMARY: Yes. The sun has been in it since six this morning. Have you seen Philip?

TONY: I've slept in it for fifteen years.

ROSEMARY: Do you know where Philip is?

TONY: I expect he's talking to mother.

ROSEMARY: Oh. Well, they're very old friends, aren't they?

TONY: Inseparable. They started quarrelling this morning at seven o'clock.

ROSEMARY: What about? I thought Philip had gone for a walk?

TONY: They both went for a walk. Around and around the garden. Quarrelling.

ROSEMARY: But what about?

TONY: Politics.

ROSEMARY: Oh.

TONY: These people talk about politics with all the passionate intensity other people reserve for sex. Extraordinary.

ROSEMARY: I didn't know Philip was interested in politics.

TONY: Are you?

ROSEMARY: I've never thought about it. And you?

TONY [*after a pause*]: No.

ROSEMARY: I really must talk to Philip [*turning back upstairs*].

TONY: Don't go. Stay and talk to me.

ROSEMARY: What about?

TONY: Just talk.

ROSEMARY [*going back out of sight*]: Perhaps he's gone back to our room.

TONY [*looking round*]: Oh God what a *mess*! [*He leaps up, makes an ineffectual attempt to clear papers, etc. His eyes fall on the looking-glass; he goes over, is about to take it off the wall when* MYRA *comes into sight at the top of the stairs. She is wearing her old trousers and sweat-shirt, is unmade-up, and has a cigarette between her lips.*]

MYRA: What are you doing?

TONY [*into the mirror*]: Peekaboo.

MYRA: What are you doing?

TONY: What's this looking-glass doing here?

MYRA: Well, why not?

TONY [*pointing at place over divan*]: It's always hung there.

MYRA: Has it? Oh, do leave it alone, Tony.

TONY [*leaving it, returning to the divan*]: It's always hung here.

MYRA: Oh. Yes, I remember when you came back from school you always used to go all over the house to see if everything was in the same place. [*She laughs.*]

TONY [*anxious and querulous*]: Every time I go away, when I come back it's as if a bomb's exploded in it – why is every-thing in such a *mess*, Mother?

MYRA [*impatiently, as she begins to strip the divan and make it*]: Oh, I haven't time. I get bored with all these *things*. They just accumulate and pile up ... When I think I once swore I would never own *things*, I'd never accumulate possessions – and now I've lived in one house for fifteen years and I feel it's sitting all over me like a – toad!

TONY [anxious, following her around]: Mother, how can you say
that — we've always lived here.

MYRA: Always! I would never have believed once that I'd live
in one place for fifteen years — it's disgusting. I'll be so pleased
to be rid of it.

TONY: Rid of it? You don't mean that?

MYRA: I do.

TONY: Mother, but what's disgusting is that it's such a *mess*.
Lord, everything's in a mess. Even the front door lock is
broken.

MYRA: Oh, what does it matter!

TONY: Oh, I'm sure *that* appeals to you: Walk right in, walk
right in, ladies and gentlemen, the humanitarian conscience
is always at home and waiting.

MYRA [*pushing him out of her way*]: Oh, Tony, when I do try
and clear up ... Why don't you put some clothes on? Or
are you trying to get a glamorous tan?

TONY [*in disgust*]: Oh, Jesus! [*He drags his black sweater on over
his pyjama coat.*] Well, how's the happy couple this morning?

MYRA: How should I know?

TONY: But you've been in animated conversation with Uncle
Philip for hours.

MYRA [*grinning*]: I naturally didn't mention Rosemary — that
would be in such bad taste.

TONY: You must have gathered through your antennae, so to
speak, how things were going — no? Well, I'd like to know.
They are sitting gazing into each other's eyes? Or perhaps
they've gone back to bed. *My* bed. My well-warmed bed.
First Sandy. Then Uncle Philip and Rosemary.

MYRA [*grimly amused*]: Philip asked me if I had another bed I
could put into their room. So I did. Twin beds side by side
like an advertisement in an American magazine. I felt so
much better. [*She laughs.*]

TONY: I can't think why.

MYRA: Philip and I shared a three-foot bed for five years.

TONY: *Do you have to?*

MYRA: Yes, I do. *That he should bring her here.* God, men are
the end. They really are the end.

TONY: Uncle Philip is probably not aware of your enduring passion for him.

MYRA: He's very well aware of it. *Ergo.*

TONY: *Ergo* what?

MYRA: Well, let's see what happens. [*She kicks* TONY'S *shoes out of the way.*]

[TONY, *irritated, jumps across, puts on his shoes, returns to the floor.*]

TONY: If you go on being so charming to that poor girl she might permanently lose her powers of speech.

MYRA [*genuinely upset*]: But, Tony, I was doing my best. I really was.

TONY: Last night at dinner you were like Beatrice Lillie impersonating – our dear queen.

MYRA: What do you want me to do – burst into tears?

TONY: Why not, if you feel like it? Why don't you ever?

MYRA: I do my crying in private. Do you imagine, after putting up such a good show with Philip all this time, I'm going to behave like a jilted 16-year-old? Obviously not.

TONY: Oh, obviously.

MYRA: What I can't stand is the damned dishonesty of it. Men are so dishonest.

TONY: I'm sure you're right. But why in this case?

MYRA [*impatiently*]: Oh, surely you can see? He doesn't want to marry her. But he hasn't got the guts to do it himself, so he brings her here. He never did have any guts. I was manoeuvred into a position where I had to break it off or lose my self-respect. And that's what he's doing with her. Bloody man.

TONY [*languidly*]: And why do you love such a despicable person?

MYRA: Oh – love. I never use the word.

TONY: I do.

MYRA: I wish you would.

TONY: When it means nothing?

MYRA [*laughs. But she is not far off tears*]: Oh, don't be so solemn. Can't you ever laugh? You're such a boring lot. The young

are so boring. I've come to the conclusion I can't stand the
company of anyone under the age of 35.

TONY: You mean you can't stand the company of the uncor-
rupted?

MYRA [amused]: Wh-at?

TONY: I've spent a good part of what are known as my forma-
tive years listening to the conversation of the mature. You
set my teeth on edge. You're corrupt. You're sloppy and
corrupt. I'm waiting for that moment when you put your
foot down about something and say you've had enough. But
you never do. All you do is watch things – with interest. If
Philip murdered Rosemary, seduced Sandy and stole all your
money, all you'd say would be: How interesting!

MYRA: He'd murder me, not Rosemary. Obviously.

TONY: Oh, obviously, obviously, obviously. That would be
interesting, wouldn't it?

MYRA [grimly amused]: It's so hard for a man when his wife dies
and leaves him unprotected!

TONY: I thought you liked his wife.

MYRA: I did. But alas, she's dead. Some men stay married
because it protects them against the – necessity of marrying
somebody else. Philip married her when she was 20, and
after that they hardly saw each other. He was very fond of
her – as the phrase goes. And so he should have been. She
lived like a nun on a mountain peak, forgiving him his sins,
and from time to time he returned to the *good* woman for a
nice rest. But now she's dead. So there's Rosemary. The
moment I heard Philip's wife was dead, I said to myself.
'Ah-ha,' I said, 'he's going to be in trouble with Rosemary
before the year's out.'

TONY: I thought you'd never heard of Rosemary.

MYRA: Rosemary, Felicity, Harriet. What does it matter? Of
course he doesn't want to marry her. So he brings her here,
where she's thoroughly lost and humiliated. [turning on him]
God, you are a cowardly hypocritical lot.

TONY [languidly]: Why me? You forget I haven't started using
the word 'love' yet.

MYRA [grimly]: I've no doubt you soon will. But I'm not going to cope with the sacrifices to your vanity — I'm not. You can manage them yourself.

TONY: Well, if you understand it all . . . if you understand it . . . [*He falls back on the floor.*] *You* understand it so that's enough.

MYRA: But I'm not blaming anyone for anything. It seems to me, as far as sex is concerned, or if you prefer it, love, the only thing to do is to shrug your shoulders [*she shrugs her shoulders*] and forgive everyone.

TONY: But you haven't forgiven Philip.

MYRA: No.

TONY: Do be nice to that poor girl. It's like seeing a poor little fly being hypnotized by a horrible brown spider.

MYRA: Poor little fly.

TONY: Can't you really see that she's terrified of you?

MYRA [*really surprised*]: Of me?

TONY: You've just explained to me why she should be.

MYRA: It's humiliating for both of us. But *frightened* — of *me*? [*She goes to the looking-glass and looks at herself.*] She's 20.

TONY: Then for God's sake why don't you at least make up your face? I really can't stand it, seeing you slop around the house half the day looking like that.

MYRA: When I'm cleaning the house I expect to be loved for myself.

TONY: Why do you have to clean it? [*as she does not reply, but begins to hum to herself*] Oh, all right, be a martyr. But I don't enjoy housework so don't expect me to slump about on my knees.

MYRA: I haven't asked you to. [*She has finished the divan and now bundles objects into the cupboard haphazard.*]

TONY: What interests me much more than the convolutions of your emotions and Uncle Philip's is Rosemary. Why does a girl of 20 want to marry a jaded old — uncle. The newspapers say it's the thing these days. One marries a man old enough to be your father. Why?

MYRA: I thought you didn't read the newspapers.

TONY: Why? Because he has *experience*? Is that it? [*in disgust*] Jesus!

MYRA: Philip has always been attractive to women

TONY: Attractive! When I was doing my time in his office I was permanently amazed at the way all the women were ready to lie down and let him walk all over them. Why? Well, you did too, didn't you? So you can explain it to me.

MYRA: I dare say they are under the impression that older men are kinder than young ones.

TONY: *Kinder!* This morning I heard Rosemary say: 'Darling, don't you love me any more?' and he said: 'Darling, you're simply being hysterical.' [MYRA *turns away sharply.*] Well, did he tell you you were hysterical?

MYRA [*breaking down and crying for a few seconds before pulling herself together*]: Tony, have some pity on me sometimes.

TONY [*appalled*]: Pity? Me? But you're not crying, are you?

MYRA: No. [*She begins rubbing a cleaner over the boards around the carpet.*] No.

TONY: I should think not.

MYRA: If Philip's off to the office then I suppose we'll have to entertain Rosemary. Of course I can always rely on you. Thank God, there's Sandy.

TONY: Yes, thank God for Sandy. He can always be relied upon to cope with any social situation. Where is he?

MYRA: Working in my room, I suppose. We've got that big meeting tomorrow night.

TONY: So interesting how that boy's turned out. Who would have foreseen this idealism in Sandy? [MYRA *stands still, leaning on the cleaner.*] What's the matter?

MYRA: Giddy. No, leave me alone.

TONY: You're not still having the change of life, are you?

MYRA: No, dear. As you know, I've finished with it.

TONY: How should I know? [*muttering*] Change of life, change of life. Well, you haven't changed much.

MYRA: Tony, will you do me a small favour? Keep out of my way just for a couple of days.

TONY: I could move into Uncle Mike's flat.

MYRA: Oh, do anything you like.

TONY: If your sense of timing hadn't been wrong, and I had been coming home next week, what would I have found?

Sandy back with Milly and a nice empty house and you all ready to entertain me.

MYRA: You know quite well you didn't let me know – just so as to catch me out.

TONY [*pathetically*]: Couldn't you really remember the date I was to finish?

MYRA: Oh, Tony, why should I? Any normal person would have let me know. It's been two years. You've been popping back and forth from camp for two years. It's a long time.

TONY: So you'd like me to move into that flat for a week?

MYRA: But you know I wouldn't. Why do you think I want to get rid of you? I thought you'd want to live by yourself.

TONY: But why?

MYRA: It's normal for a young man to want to live by himself, isn't it?

TONY: Then I'm obviously not normal.

MYRA: I was making it easy for you – that's all. I've told Mike you definitely don't want the flat.

TONY: Easy for me?

MYRA [*embarrassed*]: Well . . . in case you felt you ought to stay with me when you didn't want to.

TONY: Ought to? Why?

MYRA [*giving him a long incredulous look*]: Well, I don't know. [*pause*] I do wish Milly would come back.

TONY: Why?

MYRA: She's so kind.

TONY: Kind, kind! You've got Sandy, haven't you? Isn't Sandy kind?

MYRA: You're a lot of savages. The young are a lot of savages.

TONY: Then why – oh, don't tell me. Of course – he's good in bed. Is that it?

MYRA [*smoothly*]: Oh, he's very accomplished. Very. [*irritated*] He's *so* efficient. My dear, there are times when I feel I should be clapping.

TONY: Don't tell me that's not enough. Then *why*?

MYRA [*grinning*]: Vieillesse oblige.

TONY: That smooth-faced well-mannered little spiv. I should have thought that Sandy was everything you hated. He'll

end up as Master of the Queen's Wardrobe. Or Personnel
Manager for the Federation of Imperial Industries. Something
needing *tact*. Tact. Tact. Tact. Well, it's no use your trying
to be tactful, Mother. Who's been alerted to talk to me?
Sandy? Is it dear Uncle Sandy? Or is it Uncle Philip?

MYRA [*grinning*]: Well, actually, it's Philip.

TONY [*grinning*]: What's the plot?

MYRA: You see, it's like this . . .

[PHILIP *and* ROSEMARY *come into view on the staircase.*]

ROSEMARY [*kissing him*]: Good-bye, darling.

PHILIP: Good-bye, darling.

ROSEMARY: Darling, you've forgotten your briefcase. [*They go
back out of sight.*]

TONY [*grinning*]: He's forgotten his briefcase. Well, Mother?

MYRA: The idea was that he would handle you for me – I
suggested he should take you back into his office. No, Tony,
do wait a minute. It's your whole future at stake.

TONY: Yes, it's *my* future.

MYRA: It would take you six months to study for that exam-
ination.

TONY: A year, after my brain's gone to pot in the army.

MYRA: Ohhh – do stop being so sorry for yourself all the time.

PHILIP'S VOICE ABOVE: Good-bye, darling.

ROSEMARY'S VOICE: Good-bye, darling.

PHILIP'S VOICE: Good-bye.

TONY: Oh, *Christ*! It really is repulsive, you must admit. [*as*
MYRA *shrugs*] All right, it's all very beautiful and holy. Mother
– when I left Philip's office before, it was because I couldn't
stand it.

MYRA: Couldn't stand what?

TONY: Seeing Uncle Philip and his admiring staff, his willing
harem.

[PHILIP *comes into sight at top of the stairs.*]

MYRA: Oh, you impossible bloody little *prig*. [*She stands at
window, back turned, furious.*]

TONY: [*talking up as* PHILIP *comes down*]: Uncle Philip, mother has left us alone for the interview.

PHILIP [*preoccupied*]: Yes. It's about this job. I expect she told you.

TONY: Thanks, I don't want it. Mother, interview over [*goes to the divan, flings himself on it*].

MYRA [*coming fast across to* PHILIP]: Oh, Philip, can't you . . .

[PHILIP *shakes his head gently at her, smiles, offers her a cigarette. They smile and shrug.*]

TONY: Songs without words.

PHILIP: I must be getting along to the office. It's really very good of you to have Rosemary here, Myra.

MYRA [*laughing*]: I think so, too.

PHILIP [*embarrassed*]: Yes, well. [MYRA *laughs again. He suddenly leans forward and kisses her cheek. She kisses his.*]

MYRA [*amused*]: You know you can always count on me for anything.

PHILIP: Yes.

MYRA: Dear Philip.

PHILIP: I really must hurry.

MYRA: But I want to ask you something. It's about Max. You remember Max?

PHILIP: Well, of course. You mean the Max from the International Brigade?

MYRA: He's in trouble.

PHILIP: Who isn't?

MYRA: He's been blacklisted in America and he'd like a temporary job to tide him over.

PHILIP: But I don't need script-writers in my office. Well, what are his qualifications?

MYRA: He's an awfully nice person.

PHILIP [*laughing*]: All right, send him along.

MYRA: Philip, I suppose you wouldn't like to be one of the sponsors for a new protest we're getting up?

PHILIP [*cautiously*]: A protest against what?

MYRA: I'll explain.

[*The* TWO *of them are standing very close together by the window* R, *looking into each other's faces.* ROSEMARY *comes slowly down the stairs. She has been crying. They do not notice her.*]

PHILIP: Myra dear, I don't know how often I've told you that I don't believe in this – you can do more by quietly pulling strings than you ever can by mass protests and committees and that kind of thing.

MYRA: Since when have you told me! Yesterday. So now you believe in pulling strings. What's happened to you, Philip? What has happened? You used to be a Socialist.

PHILIP [*drily*]: I've discovered that I was a Socialist because I believed in liberty, freedom, democracy. [*laughs*] Well, Myra?

[ROSEMARY, *who has been waiting for* PHILIP *to see her, looks at* TONY. *He pats the divan beside him. She sits by him. They sit side by side, in the same listless pose, listening.*]

[*tenderly*] Myra dear, do you really imagine that any Government in the world cares about the protests of nice-minded human-itarians?

MYRA: They care about having pressure put on them. I've got a list as long as my two arms of people in prison, sentenced to death, deported, banned, prohibited, blacklisted . . .

PHILIP: Which side of the world this time? Ours or theirs?

MYRA: Ours.

PHILIP: And what about Dimitri?

MYRA: No. Oh, no . . . I thought he was out of prison.

PHILIP: I had a letter from Willi yesterday. He says Dimitri died in prison. Of course now he's officially rehabilitated and a hero of the people.

MYRA: Torture?

PHILIP: I suppose so. Probably. [*putting his arm round her*] Don't cry. What's the use? [*ironically*] Besides, he's died for socialism, hasn't he?

TONY: Don't let yourself be misled. They're talking about socialism in Russia, not Britain. It's tearing them apart, the way people are nasty to each other – in Russia.

MYRA: I can't stand your cynicism. I never could stand it.

PHILIP: You'd better stick to your Hydrogen Bomb. Stick to disarmament.

MYRA: You mean that we've got to accept the fact that in our time there's not going to be democracy, there's not going to be freedom, there's not going to be liberty?

PHILIP: Yes, of course. Who cares about liberty? The *people*? [*laughs bitterly*].

TONY [*to* ROSEMARY]: One half of this lot are bogged down emotionally in the thirties with the Spanish Civil War, and the other half came to a sticky end with Hungary. If you cut them open you'd find Spain or Hungary written in letters of blood on their soft heart — but not Britain. Certainly not poor old Britain.

PHILIP [*with an eye on* TONY, *to* MYRA]: Why don't you recognize the fact that we've had it? We've served our purpose.

MYRA: You mean we should leave it all to the youth? God help us, all they care about is . . .

PHILIP: I'm late. See you later, Myra [*goes out hastily R*].

TONY [*to* MYRA]: Yes, why don't you recognize the fact that you've had it?

MYRA [*irritably, to* TONY *and* ROSEMARY]: If we stop do-gooding and just sit back with our feet up, are you going to take over? [*looking at their listless poses*] God, you are a petty, respectable little lot.

TONY [*facing her*]: Mother.

MYRA: Well?

TONY: I gather that at the moment your large heart is full of pity for the victims of *capitalist* witch-hunts.

MYRA: And why shouldn't it be? What are you trying to say?

TONY [*laughing*]: That's all.

MYRA: You could make out a case for the whole lot of us being so discredited, so morally discredited, that we should all take a unanimous decision to stay quiet for the rest of our lives. [*He does not reply.*] We should acknowledge our total failure and leave everything in your hands. In the hands of the glorious battling youth whose banners are unsmirched. If you had any banners, that is.

TONY [*shouting*]: You're so damned self-righteous.

MYRA: I don't feel self righteous. Of course if we did retire gracefully from the field, you'd lose the benefit of our really rather unique experience.

TONY: Unique. All your lot have proved is that every political party lies and its members lie to themselves. Did that really need proving?

MYRA: What are you saying then? What is it that you want me to say?

TONY: I wonder how many people died in torture and misery and starvation during the years 1935 to 1939 while you stood on platforms smiling prettily and talking about democratic socialism.

MYRA: Yes, I know.

TONY: I wish I had a tape-recording of some of your speeches during that time. Well?

MYRA: What is it that you want me to say? Do you want me to give up – like Philip? Philip's going to become a nice kind-hearted business man giving money to good causes – Oh, God, *no*. [*remembering* ROSEMARY] Of course, he is a wonderful architect . . . Tony, I do wish you'd think about Philip's offer. You aren't really going to be an electrician, are you? [*humorously, to* ROSEMARY] Tony's going to be an electrician. He's quite determined to be. What do you think?

ROSEMARY [*fiercely*]: I think people ought to be what they want to be.

TONY: Hurray, Rosemary's on my side.

ROSEMARY: Mother wanted me to be a doctor, but I wanted to be a nurse.

TONY: Luckily Uncle Philip enjoys very good health for a man of his age. [*at* MYRA'S *angry look*] Well, he does, doesn't he?

ROSEMARY [*politely*]: Why do you want to be an electrician?

TONY: Perhaps I'll be a telephone engineer. Mother, did you know I could be a telephone engineer? Communications, that's the thing. Bringing people together. Mother, do you suppose if we talked to each other on the telephone it would be easier? We could go into different rooms and talk to each other – or play each other little items from your tape-recorder . . . [*imitates the sound of machine-gun fire*]

MYRA: Oh, damn you. What do you want? Is it that you want me to give up the H-Bomb work, is that it?

TONY: Well, of course not. Of course you should go on about the bomb. Or, as you usually refer to it – your bomb. Why, I might even help you with it.

MYRA: Then I don't know, I really don't.

TONY: The simple fight for survival – we're all in on that. But what for? Or don't you ask yourself any more? [*She shrugs impatiently.*] Why are you sitting there looking so tortured? You've got what you wanted, haven't you? Well? You've spent your life fighting for socialism. There it is, socialism. You said you wanted material progress for the masses. God knows there is *material* progress. Hundreds of millions of people progressing in leaps and bounds towards a materially-progressive heaven.

MYRA: Are you pleased about it or are you not?

TONY: Of course I'm pleased. Down with poverty. By the way, Mother, have you ever actually seen poverty? The real thing, I mean. I haven't. Well, have you? [*to* ROSEMARY] Have you, Rosemary?

ROSEMARY: My family aren't very well off.

TONY: Rosemary knows all about it. Hurray! In Britain people wear poverty like a medal around their necks – a sign of virtue. We aren't very well off! Mother, do you realize you've spent your whole life fighting to end something you know nothing about?

MYRA [*irritated to the point of tears*]: Would you please be kind enough to tell me what it is you want, then?

TONY: Do you know what it is you've created, you and your lot? What a vision it is! A house for every family. Just imagine – two hundred million families – or is it four hundred million families? To every family a front door. Behind every front door, a family. A house full of clean, well-fed people, and not one of them ever understands one word anyone else says. Everybody a kind of wilderness surrounded by barbed wire shouting across the defences into the other wildernesses and never getting an answer back. That's socialism. I suppose it's progress. Why not? To every man his wife and two children and a chicken in the pot on Sundays. A beautiful picture — I'd die for it. To every man his front door and his front door key. To each his own wilderness. [*He pauses for breath.*] Well?

MYRA: If you're going to put all that energy into dreaming dreams why don't you dream to some purpose?

TONY: Dreams, dreams, dreams — like your lot did? What are the words — don't say I've forgotten them, they've been stuffed down my throat all my life — liberty, democracy, brotherhood — and what's that other one? Ah, yes, comradeship, that's it. A world full of happy brothers and comrades.

MYRA: Does that really seem so silly?

TONY: Jesus, you aren't actually sitting there and telling me you still believe in — *Jesus!* [*to* ROSEMARY] Do you know, this lot still believe in it! What do you think?

ROSEMARY: I think I believe that people should be kind to each other.

TONY [*roaring with laughter*]: There, Mother, Rosemary's on your side — she believes people should be nice to each other.

[MYRA, *seeing* ROSEMARY *is hurt, puts out her hand to* ROSEMARY'S *arm —* ROSEMARY *twitches away.*]

MYRA [*to* TONY]: So many people have died for it. Better people than you.

TONY: *Died.* [*laughs*]

MYRA: Just imagine, during the last fifty years hundreds of thousands of people have died in torture and in loneliness, believing they were dying for the future — for *you* Tony.

TONY: [*furious*]: Well, it doesn't mean anything to me. All your damned hierarchy of Socialist martyrs — what bloody right had they to die for me? Bullying, that's what it is. I'm not going to have your holy dead hung around my neck. [*to* ROSEMARY] Do you realize what it is they are saying? Because hundreds of thousands of Socialist martyrs took it upon themselves to die for a world full of happy brothers and comrades, we've got to fall into line. Well, what do you say?

ROSEMARY: I don't know — my parents weren't political.

TONY: Oh, aren't you lucky!

MYRA: Tony, please tell me — what is it that you want? You must want something?

TONY: To be left alone, that's all. And I don't want any more suffering — no more fighting and suffering and dying. What for? Oh, the great company of martyrs who went singing to the stake and the thumbscrews and the firing-squads for the sake of the noble dream of ever-fuller wage packets and a chicken in every pot. To each man his own front door — to each man his own — refrigerator! [roars with laughter]

[ROSEMARY suddenly bursts into tears. MYRA tries to put her arms around her. ROSEMARY tears herself away and runs upstairs.]

MYRA: Oh, Tony, do you have to.

TONY [deflated and miserable]: But I was talking to you. What does she have to cry for?

MYRA: I dare say the poor girl was upset by your happy picture of the world.

TONY: I didn't mean to make her cry. What shall I do?

MYRA: You could go upstairs and be nice to her.

TONY: Be nice to her. Say I'm sorry.

MYRA: Oh, do I have to tell you what to do? Go upstairs and put your arms around her.

TONY: I put my arms around her and then she'll feel fine.

MYRA: Really, is it such a hard thing to do — to go upstairs to that poor child and be warm and nice to her?

TONY: Yes, it is. Oh, very well, if you want me to. [He stands as if waiting to be ordered.]

MYRA [shrugging]: If I want you to.

TONY: Therapy for soul-trouble, a man's arms.

[The door bell rings, R.]

MYRA: Oh, no.

TONY: Perhaps it's Philip. Well, he can go and put his arms around her. [Goes out R. MYRA lets herself slump on the divan, eyes closed. TONY comes back.]

MYRA: Who is it? I'm not in.

TONY: I'll give you three guesses . . . It's Milly.

MYRA [jumping up, radiating joy]: Milly, now?

TONY: You're surely not pleased? Now Sandy'll have to go back to his mum.

MYRA: Oh, don't be so stupid. [*goes fast towards R*] Where is Milly? [*to* TONY] Oh, get upstairs to that child, be a man for once in your life, can't you?

TONY: All right, I'm going. [*goes obediently to stairs*]

MYRA: And could you please keep your jolly little tongue off Milly for a time? She's been traipsing back and forth across the world and she'll be tired.

TONY: Perhaps you'd like me to put my arms around her, too. Perhaps I should make love to Milly. Would it be good for her – soothing after her travels? Or good for me?

MYRA: Oh, Tony, don't take it out of Milly.

[*The door opens R and* MILLY *comes in. She is a large, firm-fleshed Yorkshire woman with a stubborn face and a practical manner. She wears her hair tight back in a firm chignon. Her voice is Yorkshire. She is beaming.*]

MILLY: Well, love, I'm back.

MYRA [*kissing her*]: Oh, Milly, I've never been so pleased to see anyone.

MILLY: Me, too. A delegation of twenty women for two weeks – not my idea of fun and games. I changed to an earlier plane and here I am.

MYRA: Milly, darling, you look marvellous. Tell me about Japan. Tell me about everything. Come and sit down and talk. We'll have a party. Yes, of course, that's what we must do. We'll have a party.

TONY [*disgusted, from the stairs*]: Oh, no, no, no, no, no.

### CURTAIN

# Act Two

## SCENE 1

*The stage is semi-darkened.* TONY *is lying on the divan, wearing his black cord trousers, but nothing on above the waist.*
*The radio is playing an erotic tango.*
TONY *is making machine-gun noises like a small boy. His movements are all tense and anxious. Throughout the first part of the scene, that is until he leaves* MILLY *and* MYRA *together, he is in that state of hysteria where one is compulsively acting a part, knows it, hates oneself for it, but can't stop.*
*The door R held tight by a chair wedged under the handle. There is loud knocking on this door.* TONY *runs across, opens with a flourish, shows his disappointment when he sees who it is.*
MYRA *enters dressed for the party and looking beautiful. She is carrying bottles for the party.*

MYRA: What's the matter, Tony?
   [*He replaces the chair under the handle.*]
   Are you ill? What's wrong?
TONY: Now why should I be ill?
MYRA: Then why are you skulking in the dark, barricaded in?
TONY: This is now my bedroom.
MYRA: Oh, I see.
TONY: How many people have you got?
MYRA: About twenty, I suppose.
TONY: You blow up a party of twenty people at a couple of hours' notice?
MYRA: Some of the people who went to Japan with Milly came back this afternoon. What's that palm-court music for? What's this all about?
TONY: Milly. I'm going to seduce Milly.

MYRA [irritated]: Why can't you seduce Milly another time? I want her to help me cut sandwiches. [*She is on her way out L.*]

TONY [*in a Boyer voice*]: Darling, I love you.

MYRA [*irritated, but troubled*]: Tony, please stop it. I do wish you'd stop it.

TONY [*as before*]: Darling, I love you.

MYRA [*furious*]: Ohh . . . I was probably wrong not to believe in corporal punishment for children.

[*She goes out L into living-room. There is a burst of music and laughter and talk from the party as she does so. As* TONY *is returning to the divan, another knock on the door, R.* TONY *opens it, admits* SANDY, *showing exaggerated disappointment when he sees who it is.*]

TONY: Oh, *no* [*wedges the chair back again*].

SANDY: What's wrong, are you ill?

TONY: Didn't you see the notice? I take it for granted that I'm invisible, that I'm simply something people walk through, but surely you saw the notice?

SANDY: What notice?

TONY: A large notice reading: No Admittance, use Tradesmen's Entrance.

SANDY: No.

TONY [*opening door to living-room, through a burst of music and talk*]: Mother, Mother!

MYRA'S VOICE: What?

TONY: Did you take down my notice?

MYRA'S VOICE: Oh, was that your notice?

TONY: I'm going to put it back.

MYRA'S VOICE: Oh, do anything you damned well like.

TONY [*shuts living-room door. Music, etc., stops*]: Everyone comes in, but simply everyone, as if my bedroom were – the hall. But not Milly, for whom I'm lying in wait.

SANDY [*blandly*]: And why are you lying in wait for my mother?

TONY [*in Boyer voice*]: I love her. The scene is set for seduction.

SANDY: Rather obviously so, perhaps. Why this cloistral gloom?

TONY [*instantly switching on more light*]: If you say so. You should know. [*in Boyer voice*] Darling, I love you. No, that doesn't sound right. [*trying again*] Darling, I love you. How's that?

SANDY: Is it true that Philip's looking for a personnel manager?

TONY [*stares. Gives his loud laugh*]: Yes. And I turned his kind offer down. It's all yours, Sandy.

SANDY: I thought I might discuss it with him. [*He proceeds L towards living-room.*]

TONY: And Mike's looking for you to see when you can start in with the Labour Party. The people wait, Sandy, they wait.

SANDY: Yes, I must discuss the whole thing with them both.

TONY: Darling, I love you. But it's no use. She'll simply go on cutting bread and butter. My body will be carried past her on a shutter and . . . I was born out of my time. Yes, I've suddenly understood what my tragedy is. I was born out of my time.

SANDY: Why don't you offer to help her cut the sandwiches? [*goes into living-room accompanied by a burst of music, etc.*]

TONY [*striking his forehead with his fist*]: Clown, I never thought of it.

[*A knock on the door R. TONY opens it with a flourish, shows exaggerated delight as MILLY comes in. She is wearing a black sweater that leaves her shoulders bare. She drops her coat on a chair.*]

Wait, I must hang up my notice [*goes out R*].

MILLY [*after him through the door*]: What notice?

TONY [*returning*]: There, we shall be undisturbed. [*Wedges the door again. Advances on her purposefully.*] But your shoulders, Milly, your shoulders, my eyes dazzle.

MILLY: What are you up to, young Tony?

TONY: I'm seducing you. [*kisses her shoulder*] There. Can I help you cut the sandwiches?

MILLY: What are you seducing me for?

TONY: Oh . . . to redress certain balances. [*pulls her towards him*] Besides, mother says I must.

MILLY [*amiably*]: Well, this is a surprise.

TONY: That's not what you should have said.

MILLY [*going calmly towards L*]: Perhaps another time. Where is my son?

TONY: You shouldn't ask that either

MILLY: Is he coming home tonight or not? Because if not, one of the people I came back with on the plane could use his room.

TONY: You are a disgusting lot of women. [*puts his arms around her from behind and bites her ear*]

MILLY: Mind, I don't want to have to do my hair again . . .

TONY: You should slap my face. Then I should slap yours. Then we should fall on the bed.

MILLY: But I haven't got time. And you don't know what you're doing, inviting a punch from me. My husband hit me the once. [*shows him a large and efficient fist*]

TONY: Then I am afraid I am nonplussed. Doesn't that music do anything to you?

MILLY: What music? Oh – that. I've got so I never hear the radio or the telly. [*is about to open door*]

TONY [*in Boyer voice*]: I love you. [MILLY *does not turn.*] I loo-ve you.

[MILLY *slowly turns, stands looking at him, hands on hips.* TONY *stares at her, derisive, rude, insulting.*]

MILLY [*quietly*]: What you're going to get from me, young Tony, is a damned good spanking.

[TONY *suddenly collapses into tired appeal, makes a helpless gesture.*]

MILLY [*in a different voice, warm and maternal*]: You take it easy, love. You just let up and take it a bit easier.

[MYRA *comes in from L. The* TWO WOMEN *stand side by side, looking at him.*]

MYRA [*irritated*]: Do put something on, Tony. You'll catch cold.

TONY [*instantly reverting to his previous aggressiveness*]: I know, and then you'll have to nurse me. [*drags on his black sweater*]

MILLY [*easily*]: Eh, but he's a fine figure of a boy, that Tony.

MYRA: One sees such a lot of it. [*to* TONY] For God's sake, turn off that mush.

TONY [*turning off radio*]: I have failed. I have failed utterly.

MILLY: I want a large whisky. You'd better have one too, Myra.

TONY: And me too. Oh, I see. You want me to go away. Why can't I stay? I might learn something. [MYRA *and* MILLY *are arming themselves with stiff drinks.*] Mother, I thought you wanted Milly to help with the sandwiches. Why don't you both go and cut the sandwiches?

MYRA: I've finished the sandwiches.

TONY [*shrill and anxious*]: You'll be tight and giggly before the thing even starts. [*to* MYRA] Mother, you get giggly when you're tight. I really do hate to see women drink at all. [*to* MILLY, *as* MYRA *ignores him*] Do you, or do you not think I'm sexually attractive?

MILLY [*amiably but a trifle impatient*]: You're a knockout, love. [*to* MYRA] You've got to put me in the picture. What's this business with your Philip?

[TONY *regards them anxiously, as they settle down for a gossip.*]

MYRA: Oh, do run away, there's a good boy.

TONY: Well, I don't know, I don't really [*runs upstairs*].

[*The* TWO WOMEN *look at each other with raised eyebrows, sighing deeply.*]

MYRA: What am I going to do with him?

MILLY: Let me get some alcohol inside me if we are going to discuss the youth. Personally I think we should let the younger generation sink or swim without any further comment from us. [*takes a hearty swig*] They're only doing it to attract our attention.

MYRA: What's the good of sending one's son to a progressive school if he turns out like this? The idea was he'd be an integrated personality.

MILLY: Integrated with *what*?

MYRA: Ye-ees.

MILLY: Look what a public school did for Sandy.

MYRA: Hmmm. It did what it is supposed to do, surely.

MILLY: I walked out on Sandy's father because he was such a

slick little go-getter, but one can't walk out on one's son.

MYRA: One doesn't even want to. Queer.

MILLY: Very, yes. [*There is a pause; they look at each other, eyeing each other ironically.*] He's not playing you up, is he?

MYRA: Sandy? But Sandy has such *beautiful* manners. [*She giggles.*]

MILLY [*giggling*]: I believe you. Well, give him the boot, I would. He's got what he wants, I suppose. [*at* MYRA's *inquiring and rather hurt look*] Never in his life did my Sandy do anything that wasn't calculated.

MYRA: What, never?

MILLY: My principle with Sandy is, wait until he's worked through some situation – he's always in a better position than he was when he started. Then you know what he was after from the start. [*at sight of* MYRA's *face*] You're not going to shed any tears over my Sandy, are you? [*half-disgusted, half-admiring*] Wide boy ... Oh, I'm not saying he's not in love. But my Sandy'll always fall in love where it does him most good.

MYRA: An enviable talent.

MILLY: Not yours.

MYRA: Not yours.

[*They look at each other, grinning.*]

TOGETHER: Well, I don't know ...

[*They roar with laughter. Pause.*]

MILLY: That Philip now.

MYRA [*drily*]: He's brought his lady-love to stay here.

MILLY [*drily*]: And he's going to marry her next week?

MYRA: So it would seem.

MILLY: Eh, but you're behaving nicely.

MYRA: There's such a satisfaction in behaving well. Not that one's more subtle forms of insult don't escape them entirely. [*She laughs shrilly, almost breaks down.*]

MILLY [*quiet and shrewd*]: Myra, love, you'd better take it easy.

MYRA: Yes. [*blowing her nose*] Yes. [*very gay*] What's happened to that man of yours? What's his name? Jack?

MILLY: Jack, yes. [*They look at each other and laugh.*]

MYRA: Well?

MILLY [*giggling*]: I walked out.

MYRA: What for this time?

MILLY: But it's always the same reason. Yes, come to think of it, it is. Well, I was at his week-end cottage. I was going to marry him on the Monday week, as I recall . . . God knows what for. What's this thing we have about getting married?

MYRA [*grimly*]: I can't think.

MILLY: Yes, well.

MYRA: Oh well. [*They laugh.*]

MILLY: My man Jack. Yes. Well, I'd cleaned the cottage up all of Friday, just for the love of the thing. Cleaned it some more on the Saturday, cooked a dinner for ten people on Saturday night, and organized the vegetable garden Sunday. On Sunday afternoon Jack went off to play golf, and the little woman hung some new curtains in the living-room.

MYRA: You don't have to tell me. He came home at seven o'clock and wanted to know why your face wasn't made up.

MILLY: No, my man Jack didn't mind me in my working dirt. It wasn't that. He came home from his golf and gave me a nice kiss. Reward for hard work, as it were. Oddly enough, it always is.

MYRA [*grimly*]: Yes.

MILLY: Quite so. Well, then there were steps outside. My God, it was Mr Stent.

MYRA: Mr Stent?

MILLY: Assistant Manager. The shoes Jack will inherit.

MYRA: All right, I know. [*She groans.*]

MILLY: Suddenly Jack went into a tizzy. [*imitating a nervous flurried male voice*] 'Darling, that's Mr Stent. He can't see you like that. Do please change your dress.' [MYRA *giggles.*] I said to him: 'My man, your *property* is ready for display to anyone. But *I* have been cooking, cleaning, and digging for three days and I'm tired. Mr Stent will have to take me as I come.' Jack said – [*she imitates a nervous male voice*] – 'But darling, it will make such a bad impression.' [MYRA *is helpless with laughter.*] So I went up them stairs. I bathed. I changed. I made myself up like the Queen of Sheba. Then I went downstairs and cooked and served dinner for three. Then I entertained Mr Stent – oh, on his level, of course, keeping my tiny mind well in its place so as not to upset Mr Stent. Then I wished him a very good night. Then I wished Jack good-bye. Then I took my suitcase and walked out. I left the bill behind me. To charring eighteen hours at four shillings an hour. To buying and cooking and serving first-class dinner for ten, ten guineas. To planning and organizing vegetable garden, ten guineas. To making and hanging curtains, ten guineas. To acting as hostess to Mr Stent, five guineas. I didn't charge for my services in bed. Jack never did have a sense of humour. Besides, I didn't want to ruin him. And I asked him to make out the cheque for the Society for the Protection of the Christian British Home.

MYRA: And did he?

MILLY: Oh yes, he did. He wrote me a letter saying why hadn't I let him know I was feeling like that. [*They both laugh.*]

MYRA: You have no discrimination.

MILLY: *I* haven't.

MYRA: Oh, all right.

MILLY: I suppose one has to make do with what there is.

MYRA: I was going to volunteer to go with those people to the testing area for the bomb. You know. Well, Tony was terribly upset. I was so happy. I was under the impression that he would mind if I got killed. Then he said: 'Mother, for God's sake have a sense of proportion.' Then I understood. It wouldn't have been respectable. That was what he minded. It wouldn't have been respectable. [*laughs. Almost breaks down*]

MILLY: Myra, you must let up, you really must.

MYRA: Yes.

MILLY: Your Tony's got a heart, at least.

MYRA [*surprised*]: Tony has?

MILLY: Whereas my Sandy . . . When Sandy became a gentleman as a result of his expensive education, I was expecting him to drop me – Oh! very pleasantly of course. I was surprised when he opted to stay with me. I thought it was out of love and affection. One day I heard him saying to one of his posh friends – [*imitates* SANDY] – 'You must meet my mother, she's such a character.' Light dawned on me. I played up, you can imagine. I was a woman of the people with a heart of gold. Really, I made myself sick – revolting! I'll be an asset to him in the Labour Party, won't I? Meet my mum, a working woman with a heart of gold . . . Little – wide boy.

MYRA: Milly, Sandy's very fond of you.

MILLY: Hmmm, yes.

MYRA: Milly, why did you give him that kind of education then?

MILLY [*defensively*]: I was doing the best for him.

MYRA: Were you – well? I don't think he thinks so.

MILLY: What? What's he said to you?

MYRA: Milly, are you sure there's not a good part of you that likes Sandy the way he is?

MILLY: What's he said to you?

MYRA: He once said that you've equipped him to play the racket, and he has no choice but to play it.

MILLY: No choice. Ohhh! – so it's my fault, is it?

MYRA: Aren't our children our fault?

MILLY: No choice! [*throwing it off*] I wish you'd give him the boot before he drops you. I wish you would. It'd do him so much good.

MYRA: [*with determination*]: Very well, I shall. Sandy, I shall say, Sandy, I no longer care for you.

MILLY: And do you?

MYRA [*grinning*]: It's so nice to have a man about the house.

MILLY [*grinning*]: Yeees.

MYRA: Well, it is. [*her face changes*] What am I going to do about Tony . . . Milly, what am I going to do? [*She almost breaks down.* MILLY *comes behind her, puts her arms around her.*]

MILLY: Myra, for God's sake, stop punishing yourself . . . We've lived our lives, haven't we? And we've neither of us given in to anything. We've both of us come through not too badly, considering everything. We're not going to come to a dead end in our sons?

MYRA: No.

MILLY: What's the use of living the way we have, what's the use of us never settling for any of the little cosy corners or the little cages or the second-rate men if we simply get tired now?

MYRA: Yes.

MILLY: Were you really going out with those people to the H-Bomb tests?

MYRA: Yes.

MILLY: Because you knew the Government wouldn't let any-one get near them anyway?

MYRA: No. I really wanted to — do something.

MILLY: You didn't mind getting killed?

MYRA: No.

MILLY: Myra, love, we all of us get depressed.

MYRA: [wrenching herself away from her]: Depressed. That word annoys me. Half the time we dope ourselves up with some stimulant — men, our children, work. Then it fails and we see things straight, and it's called being depressed. You know quite well that there's only one question that everyone's asking — what are we alive for? Why? Why shouldn't that damned bomb fall? Why not? Why shouldn't the human race blow itself up? Is it such a loss? A little dirty scum on the surface of the earth — that's what we are.

MILLY [ironically]: Scum, scum — that's all.

MYRA [impatiently]: All right — laugh me out of it — it's easy enough. [laughs, irritably]

MILLY: If I remind you in a month from now of things you are saying tonight you'll laugh and say, 'Well, I was depressed then.'

MYRA: I dare say. Oh yes, I dare say. [She is in a fever of irritation, angry, laughing, stamping about the stage, deadly serious.] I keep dreaming, Milly. You know I keep having the same dream . . .

MILLY: Oh — dreams. So now we're going to turn into a pair of old women plotting our dreams and looking for portents.

MYRA: [almost growling]: Ohhh! — yes. But I do. Every time I get my head on to a pillow, it's the same thing . . .

MILLY: Oh! Lord save us – get yourself tight and be done with it.

MYRA: No! Listen to me. Listen, Milly. [*She grabs* MILLY *to make her listen.* MILLY *is ironical, sceptical, uncomfortable.*] The whole world is full of great black machines. I am standing on the surface of the earth somewhere and everywhere about me on an enormous plain are great black machines. It is a world of cold white buildings and black motionless machines . . .

MILLY: Ho-ho – so we're against the machine now, are we; back to the Golden Age!

MYRA: . . . And I'm standing there, waiting. That's what it is, Milly, we're all waiting. No, listen . . . [*Now holds* MILLY *fast, making her listen. Slowly* MILLY *succumbs, becomes part of the dream with* MYRA.] We are standing, waiting. We lift our eyes and see the curve of the horizon . . . it's on fire, Milly. Not a real fire – the curve of the earth crackles with the cold white crackle of electricity. Then we understand – the earth is burning. They've set the bomb off somewhere and half of the earth is already gone. Everywhere in front of us the plain is disintegrating in a cold white crackle of fire. It will reach us in a minute. And we stand there thinking, thank God. Thank God it's all over. Thank God it's all over . . .

[*For a minute* MILLY *is held fast inside* MYRA's *persuasiveness. She pulls away.*]

MILLY [*irritably*]: Oh! Myra . . . Well, I don't have to be asleep to see all that I can see it when I'm awake.

MYRA: [*grim and humorously desperate*]: Do you realize we've only got through half of our lives? We've got to get through another thirty or forty years of being alive – if we're unlucky.

MILLY [*with her hands over her ears*]: Shut up, shut up, Myra.

MYRA: I can't face it, Milly. I can't face another forty years of being alive.

MILLY [*uncovering her ears*]: Well, we'll both have to face it. We're both as strong as mules. [*gives* MYRA *a drink*] Now come clean, Myra. What's really eating you up? You've been talking around and around it . . . Philip's brought his girl here, Tony's in a bad mood, and it's all too much, That's all.

MYRA: That's all.

MILLY: Now listen to me. You had a good marriage with your husband. Then you and Philip were happy together for five years – that's more than most people get in their lives. You and Philip are good friends now. There's old Mike hanging around waiting for your first moment of weakness so you'll give in and marry him. You've got Tony. You're not doing too badly.

MYRA: Oh, don't be so complacent . . . don't be so damned sensible . . . you know quite well that nothing you say to me now makes any sense at all.

MILLY [*patiently*]: Yes, love, I know.

MYRA: I wish you'd do something for me. I wish you'd talk to Tony. I can never say anything to him. He imagines I want to get rid of him. It's like this. I've got hold of some money – enough to finish his studying. Now he says he doesn't want to be an architect. So I'd like him to take it and go off for a couple of years – doing as he likes, wherever he likes. He'll never be free again. He'll be 40 before he knows it. I wish I'd had five hundred pounds at his age to spend as I liked, to find out about the world. Well, if you could talk to him perhaps he might listen.

MILLY: You've raised five hundred pounds by doing your own housework?

MYRA: No, no, of course not.

MILLY: Myra, what've you been up to – what've you done?

MYRA: But I can't talk to him, Milly. He thinks I want to get rid of him.

MILLY [*holding her and forcing her to face her*]: Myra, what have you done?

MYRA: I've sold the house.

MILLY: You haven't.

MYRA: Yes, I have. To raise money for Tony.

MILLY: But, Myra, what are you going to do?

MYRA [*almost airily*]: I have no idea.

MILLY: You're going to marry old Mike.

MYRA: Oh, no. Why, Milly, I didn't expect you to be so – careful. What does it matter? I do hate being tied down. I always did. Surely it's more important for Tony to be free than to fuss about some bricks and a roof . . . if it comes to the worst you'll always take me in.

MILLY: But what's Tony going to say? Have you told him?

MYRA: Why should he care? He's young.

MILLY: Why haven't you told him?

MYRA: Because I can't talk to him.

[TONY *comes down the stairs.*]

MILLY: Look out, he's coming.

[MYRA *hastily turns away to compose her face.*]

TONY: Finished your girlish confidences? Though why it has to be in my bedroom . . .

MILLY: Why don't you choose some other place to park yourself?

MYRA: Obviously the hall is the place most calculated to cause the maximum inconvenience to everybody.

TONY: I do hope you're going to make up your face, Mother. [MYRA *goes into living-room without replying.*] What's wrong with mother?

MILLY: She's tired. [*going towards living-room*] Come on, we've got to be gay if it kills us. Aren't you coming in at all?

TONY: No.

MILLY: You aren't interested to hear what's going on in Japan?

TONY: I'm sure the people in Japan feel like people everywhere else in the world – as if they've been handcuffed to a sleeping tiger.

MILLY: I want to talk to you sometime, young Tony.

TONY [*in Boyer voice*]: I want to talk to you, too. [MILLY *goes impatiently into living-room.*]

TONY [*collapsing on the divan*]: Thank God for the silence.

[*Almost at once he starts making machine-gun noises, pointing his arm all over the room. Stops. Imitates a bomb. More machine-gun noises.* ROSEMARY *comes in fast, from living-room. She is in a party dress and looking miserable.*]

TONY: Not in a party mood?

ROSEMARY: I can't stand listening to them talk. I can't. They talk about all kinds of horrors as if they were talking about the weather.

TONY [*laughing*]: They are.

ROSEMARY: I don't see how they can be so — matter-of-fact about everything.

TONY: Don't worry about them. They were just born thick-skinned.

[ROSEMARY *sits, listlessly.* TONY *hesitates, then after a struggle with himself, sits beside her, puts his arm around her. She immediately snuggles against him and closes her eyes. There is a look on his face of incredulous but derisive pride.*]

Feeling better?

ROSEMARY: Yes. Would your mother think it rude if I left here tonight?

TONY: Don't go — unless you want to. Don't just rush away.

ROSEMARY: It was all no good. It was a mistake.

TONY: Yes, I know. Never mind. [*There is a burst of laughter and music.*]

ROSEMARY [*wistfully*]: They have a good time, don't they?

TONY: They'd have a good time if the skies were falling. If the end of the world were announced for Friday, mother would say — 'Let's have a party.'

ROSEMARY [*fiercely*]: Yes, they're so childish.

TONY: Oh God, yes ... Rosemary, I wish you'd tell me something.

ROSEMARY [*sitting up away from him*]: What — do you mean about politics — but I don't know about them.

TONY [*laughing*]: Yes, perhaps I do mean politics.

ROSEMARY: So *childish.* They talk as if they really believe what they do changes things. You know, 5,000 people listen to a speech and everything will be changed.

TONY [*laughing*]: Go on. Go on, Rosemary.

ROSEMARY: But it seems to me as if there are perhaps – six very important, very powerful men in the world – somewhere up there – we probably don't even know their names, and they make the decisions . . .

TONY: Go on.

ROSEMARY [*indicates living-room*]: In there they're talking about . . . I don't see how they can believe in it. If the 5,000 people killed themselves tomorrow in Trafalgar Square as a protest against – everything, the six powerful men up there wouldn't care, they wouldn't even notice. And it would be something in the newspapers for ordinary people.

TONY [*delighted, laughing*]: Go on, Rosemary, don't stop.

ROSEMARY: Just one of those important men can go mad or get drunk and – well, that's all. That's all.

TONY: Rosemary.

ROSEMARY: Yes. [*She lets herself fall back against him.* TONY *puts his arms around her, talks over her head.*]

TONY [*unconsciously rocking her*]: Rosemary, I've been thinking. What we need is something different. Something – very simple.

ROSEMARY [*eyes closed, against him*]: Yes.

TONY: Something very simple. I think I want to be a tramp. I've been thinking . . . the whole world is getting mass-produced and organized. But inside everybody's varnished and painted skin is a tramp. It's the inner emigration. Every morning in front of the bathroom mirror we polish our teeth and our hair and our skin, we set our faces to tick all day like metronomes against the image in the mirror until the lights go out at night. But inside, we've emigrated. We're tramps. Don't you see, Rosemary, we have to keep the tramp alive somehow. Would you like to be a tramp, Rosemary? [*Looks down at her face, but her eyes are closed. She is half-asleep.*] No, a tramp is solitary, a tramp is solitary . . . [*rocking her*] Shhh, Rosemary . . .

ROSEMARY [*sleepily*]: Yes . . .

[*The door L bursts open, letting in a shout of music and talk.* PHILIP *comes in fast,* SANDY *after him.*]

SANDY: So if you're really looking for someone perhaps you'd try me.

PHILIP [*briefly*]: Yes, of course.

SANDY: It's really awfully good of you. May I come into your office tomorrow and talk it over with you?

PHILIP [*briefly*]: Yes, do. [*to* ROSEMARY] Aren't you well?

ROSEMARY: Perfectly well, thank you. [*At her leisure she disengages herself from* TONY, *but remains sitting close beside him.*]

PHILIP: It's really very rude to run away like that. It's not polite to Myra.

ROSEMARY: I'm sure Myra will bear up.

[MYRA *comes in L, looking gay and beautiful.*]

MYRA: I can't have all the young people leaving my party. It leaves us all so dull.

SANDY [*laying his arm around her shoulders*]: Myra darling, how could any party be dull with you in it?

TONY: You should make up a Strontium-90 calypso and dance to it.

ROSEMARY: If you don't mind, Myra, I'd like to go to bed.

MYRA [*briefly*]: Of course I don't mind. [*to* TONY] I do think you might come in even if just for a few minutes.

TONY [*to* ROSEMARY]: Would you like to come out into the garden for a little? There's a moon tonight.

ROSEMARY [*with a defiantly guilty look at* PHILIP]: Yes, I'd love to . . . just for a few minutes, and then I must go to bed.

[TONY *and* ROSEMARY *go out R.* PHILIP, *after a moment, walks angrily off after them.*]

SANDY [*gracefully amused*]: Lovers' quarrels.

MYRA: Oh, quite. Charming.

SANDY: How lucky we're more sensible.

MYRA [*gaily, flirting with him*]: Dear Sandy, you're always so sensible.

SANDY: Not so sensible as to be dull, I hope.

MYRA [*mocking and affectionate*]: Dull? You? Darling, never. [*kissing him*] Darling sensible Sandy.

SANDY: Dear Myra — so sad, isn't it?

MYRA: Sad? Sad – oh, I see. [*bursts into laughter*]

SANDY [*uneasily*]: I love your laugh, darling.

MYRA: Oh, I love it too. [*regards him mockingly*]. Well, go on.

SANDY: You're in a very odd mood.

MYRA: You're quite right, darling, it's quite time for us to call it a day.

SANDY [*disconcerted*]: Yes, well, of course.

MYRA: And you've been wonderful. [*imitating him*] Sandy, you're really so *wonderful*.

SANDY [*stiffly*]: I'm so glad we are both capable of being graceful about the end. Though of course you and I are much too close ever to part, darling.

MYRA: Oh, quite so. Exactly. [*kissing him mockingly*] There. [*laughing*] I've done it. Only by the skin of my teeth though. I must tell Milly. She'll be so pleased.

SANDY: Tell her what? You haven't been discussing *us* with mother? But I'm sure she would quite agree that I did the right thing in breaking it off.

MYRA [*astounded*]: *You* did the right thing . . . [*rocking with laughter*] Why of course, yes, you did, didn't you?

SANDY [*furious*]: Really, Myra, I do think your behaviour is in very bad taste.

[*He goes angrily out R as* PHILIP *comes in from the R.*]

PHILIP: And what's wrong with your young man?

MYRA: I might ask, what's wrong with your young woman?

[*He gives a short gruff laugh. They eye each other and both laugh.*]

PHILIP: [*drily*]: Well, Myra?

MYRA: Well, Philip?

PHILIP [*with whimsical exasperation*]: Really, women, women.

MYRA: Tell me, do you find Rosemary's behaviour in bad taste?

PHILIP [*rather sentimentally*]: I suppose it is better that she should find out what I'm like before rather than after.

MYRA [*drily*]: It is *lucky*, isn't it? [*They eye each other, smiling, with an old and bitter emotion.*]

PHILIP [*on an impulse, dragged into saying it*]: It would be odd if we ended up with each other after all, wouldn't it?

MYRA [*tiredly*]: Rather odd, yes.

PHILIP [*with sentimental bitterness*]: You know me, Myra. I'm not much good . . . [*turns away, frowning – the frown is a nervous spasm of irritation against himself for the role he is playing*]

MYRA [*quickly*]: Don't do that, Philip, don't. I always did wish you wouldn't – it's so bloody insulting.

PHILIP [*gaily, but with self-dislike because he has not met her appeal*]: But, Myra, I'm proposing to you . . . I'm always proposing to you and you always turned me down.

MYRA [*ironically*]: Yes, you always were. But bigamy never did appeal to me much.

PHILIP [*half-serious, half playing at it and bitter with conflict*]: Well, old girl, what about it? Can you face all that over again?

MYRA [*against her will surrendering, smiling to him*]: What an awful prospect, all that over again . . .

[*They suddenly come together, cling together, almost kiss, passionately. But at the same moment with the same gesture of angry and bitter irritation, turn away from the embrace. They* BOTH *laugh, painfully.*]

PHILIP [*the mood of surrender is gone. They are both back in their roles. He speaks with whimsical bitterness*]: No woman ever made me as unhappy as you did. I wonder why . . .

[*She says nothing but watches him ironically.*]

MYRA: I wonder why, too.

PHILIP: I wish you'd tell me the truth now, Myra . . .

MYRA [*groaning and ironical*]: Ohhh – about my infidelities?

PHILIP [*suddenly painfully and eagerly intense*]: For instance, that American – you swore there was nothing – that he wasn't in your room that night?

MYRA [*almost groaning*]: Oh, Philip . . . do you suppose when we're both 70 you'll still be asking me . . . the one thing you can't afford to believe is that I always told you the truth.

PHILIP [*quickly*]: Oh come, come, you'll never change.

MYRA [*humorously groaning*]: Oh, Philip . . .

PHILIP [*gay, bitter, and guilty*]: After all, I can't say I don't know what I'm in for.

MYRA [*very dry*]: What you are saying is this: that you propose to marry me although you take your stand on the fact that I lied continuously to you for five years, that I was unfaithful to you for five years, and that you insist I will continue both to betray you and to lie about it.

PHILIP [*gay and guilty*]: Why, Myra dear, now that I'm older I'm more tolerant, that's all. Well, what do you say?

MYRA [*bitter, smiling*]: Obviously nothing.

PHILIP: What? [*quickly*] There you are — that's what always happens when I propose to you — you turn me down. [*She smiles at him. He smiles back. It is very painful. A moment of quiet.*] [*almost groaning*] Oh, Lord . . .

MYRA [*groaning, painful but humorous*]: Ohhh . . . [*then suddenly furious and loud*] I wish just once I could meet a man who didn't tell himself lies and expect me to believe them.

PHILIP [*shouting*]: You know quite well I can't stand the way you're always giving yourself away to everybody and everything. *I can't stand you, Myra.* [*A moment's quiet. They look at each other, smiling bitterly.*] [*whimsically*] When you've given up — when you've got grey hair and wrinkles, I'll take you on then.

MYRA: Shall I dye my hair and paint on wrinkles?

PHILIP: Yes.

MYRA: No one ever loved me as you did, no one. That's what I can't forgive you for — it wouldn't have mattered if you hadn't loved me. But you did. And you turned me down.

PHILIP [*groaning, turning away*]: Oh, let's leave it, let's leave it now.

MYRA: You turned me down because I loved you. You couldn't stand being loved.

PHILIP: Oh, Lord, it is absolutely *intolerable*!

MYRA [*between her teeth*]: Absolutely hopeless! [*They shrug, stand silent.*]

[MIKE *comes in from L.*]

MIKE: Why, here you are. Philip, where's your charming little Rosemary? Everybody's running away from the party. I thought I'd come and find you. [*comes up to* MYRA] What's

wrong, dear? [puts his arm around her] Myra dear, you really
do look bad, you know. You do really need someone to
look after you.

MYRA [letting her head lie on his shoulder] Dear Mike. You are
always so sweet.

MIKE [to PHILIP]: Myra needs someone to look after her.

PHILIP [grimly]: Perhaps she does. [with a short laugh] You two
look rather well together.

MYRA [smiling painfully to MIKE]: He thinks we look well
together. Philip does.

MIKE [wistfully]: You know what I think, dear.

MYRA [to PHILIP]: You like the sight of me and Mike together?

PHILIP [embarrassed, hurt, and angry]: Well, why not? If that's
what you want.

MYRA [to MIKE]: You'd like to take me on?

MIKE [carefully]: I don't have to tell you what I've always
wanted. [looks doubtfully from MYRA to PHILIP]

MYRA: Can you stand me, Mike? Can you stand me?

[PHILIP turns away, frowning.]

MIKE: Stand you, dear?

MYRA: It would be awful if you couldn't stand me.

MIKE: But, Myra dear, I've loved you for years. After all, I've
never made any secret of it to anybody.

[MYRA smiles at him. In an impulse of joy MIKE embraces
her. But because of her reaction the embrace ends in a brotherly
hug.]

MIKE [hopefully]: I'm so happy, dear.

MYRA: Dear Mike.

[She lays her head on his shoulder and looks at PHILIP. PHILIP
turns away with a helpless and bitter gesture. ROSEMARY and
TONY come in from garden R. They have been talking animatedly
but at the sight of the three they stop still.]

ROSEMARY [awkward because of PHILIP, to TONY]: I think I'll
go to bed now.

TONY [*forgetting* ROSEMARY *at the sight of* MIKE *and* MYRA *who still have their arms around each other*]: Well, Mother? Well, Mike?

MIKE: There you are, my boy.

ROSEMARY [*defiantly, to* PHILIP]: I must really go to bed, I'm so tired.

PHILIP [*suddenly concerned to reclaim her*]: But, Rosemary, don't go yet. Stay down here and talk a little. Have a drink.

ROSEMARY [*unwillingly reclaimed*]: Well, just for a minute – no, I won't have a drink.

[PHILIP *and* ROSEMARY *sit together on the stairs.* MYRA *and* MIKE *are standing together. His arm is still around her.*]

TONY [*looking from one couple to the other*]: Oh, no!

[MILLY *comes in from living-room.*]

MILLY: Do come and do your duty, Myra – I can't cope with all these people any longer by myself.

TONY [*fiercely to* MILLY]: Ever so interesting, sex, isn't it?

MILLY [*briskly*]: I've always found it so . . . [*but she sees his face, turns to look first at* MYRA *and* MIKE *then at* PHILIP *and* ROSEMARY]

TONY [*shrilly*]: What astounds me is the way it so obviously is everyone's favourite occupation.

MILLY [*briskly*]: Never mind, love, you'll soon get into the way of it . . . [*Looking at his face she suddenly understands he is about to crack. She lays a hand briefly on his shoulder, saying to* MIKE] Take Myra back to her guests, there's a dear.

MIKE: Of course, we're just going. [*leads* MYRA *across to living-room door. They go out*]

[MILLY *locks the door, turns to* TONY.]

TONY [*pathetically*]: She's not starting something with Mike now, is she? Surely she isn't seriously going to . . .

MILLY: And why not?

TONY [*almost beside himself, he runs to foot of the stairs and confronts* ROSEMARY]: Rosemary, come and have a drink with me, come and talk.

ROSEMARY [*taking* PHILIP *with her upstairs*]: No thanks, Tony, I think Philip and I'll go to bed now.

[PHILIP *and* ROSEMARY *go out of sight upstairs.* MILLY *jams door on R with chair.*]

TONY: Oh *no*. [*whirling on* MILLY] Why? Half an hour ago she was ready to kick dear Uncle Philip downstairs.

MILLY: Bless you, dear.

TONY: It's going to be such a jolly night. Imagine it — Rosemary and Uncle Philip in one bed — *my* bed, but let that pass. Then there's mother. Will it be Sandy or Uncle Mike, do you suppose? Why not both?

MILLY [*calmly*]: You're not talking to me about your mother like that, young Tony.

TONY [*almost ecstatic with pain*]: Or they might have a little change in the middle of the night. Mother and Uncle Philip — for old time's sake. And Sandy and Rosemary might have a good deal in common — who knows? Of course they *are* pretty near the same age, probably a handicap. Then there's you and me.

MILLY: Take it easy, Tony. Take it easy.

TONY: Three happy well-assorted couples . . . [*He roars with laughter.* MILLY, *seeing what is coming moves towards him, stands waiting.*] Three couples, each couple in a nice tidy little room with the door locked. And in the morning we'll make polite conversation at breakfast. Of course, there is an odd man out — dear Uncle Mike. Well, he can lie on the mat outside mother's door. Why shouldn't we all ring each other up in the middle of the night and report progress. The grunts and groans of pleasurable love-making would be interrupted for the sake of a few minutes' militant conversation about the dangers of the hydrogen bomb. Then back to what everyone's really interested in. It's bloody funny, when you come to think about it . . . [*He breaks down, sobbing.* MILLY *catches him as he heels over on the divan, holds him against her, rocking him.*] I simply can't stand any of it. I can't stand it. I can't stand it.

CURTAIN

# SCENE 2

*The next morning, rather early.*

*The curtain rises on the room in disorder.* MILLY *and* TONY *are lying on the untidy divan.* TONY *has his black trousers on, nothing above.* MILLY *is wearing a black lace petticoat. She is smoking and watching him with a calm maternal eye. The door L is wedged with the chair.*

TONY *makes the sound of machine-gun fire with his mouth, pointing an imaginary machine-gun over the ceiling, like a small boy.* MILLY *does not move.* TONY *does it again.*

MILLY: What's that in aid of?

TONY: I love that sound. That sound is me. I love it.

MILLY: Can't say I do.

TONY: What are you going to do when mother comes down those stairs? For God's sake put some clothes on.

MILLY: I like myself like this. Don't you?

TONY [*examines her, drops his head on his arms*]: I don't know. I don't know.

MILLY: I know. You don't. [*She caresses the back of his neck, runs the side of her palm down his spine. He shrinks away from her.*] No? [*As he remains silent, she takes his head in her arms and cradles it.*] Is this better? [*rocks him, half-tender, half-derisive*] Baby, baby, baby.

TONY: [*shutting his eyes*]: Put on some clothes. Put some clothes on.

MILLY: You'd like me to put a veil over my face and keep my hair covered.

TONY: Yes.

MILLY: Well, I'm not going to. You'd better learn to like the female form. [*rocking him*] You wanted to take me into bed so as to annoy your mother. Here I am. But when it comes to the point you're scared she might know.

TONY: She'll come down the stairs, see us and say: 'Milly, where's my H-Bomb file?'

MILLY [*laughing*]: Child. You're a child.

TONY: Oh, I can hear her. She said, 'Milly, I'm worried about that son of mine. He's still a virgin. Do something about it, will you?' Then, dismissing this item on her agenda, she said: 'Where's my tape-recording of . . .' Oh, Christ . . . [*He rolls away from her.*]

MILLY [*running the side of her palm down his spine*]: Come here, young Tony.

TONY: If you're going to seduce me again then let's have some appropriate music. [*makes machine-gun noises again*]

MILLY [*calmly, moving away from him*]: Young Tony, I'm going to give you some good advice, and if you've got any sense you'll take it.

TONY: Action. Action is what I want. Not words.

MILLY: You'll find yourself a nice friendly tart and put in a couple of weeks learning your job. Then perhaps you'll be fit for adult society.

TONY [*grinning*]: What? You're walking out on me? You've got other fish to fry? Is that it? I thought I'd found a nice friendly tart. [*She continues to regard him amiably.*] Well, why don't you hit me?

MILLY: What for?

TONY [*shrilly*]: I've insulted you.

MILLY: *You* insult *me*?

TONY: I expected you to hit me.

MILLY: Why do you want to be hit?

TONY [*collapsing on to the divan, face down*]: Oh, I don't know, I don't know, I don't know. [MILLY *lays a hand on his shoulder. He flings it off.*] [*shrilly*] I simply don't like women.

MILLY [*as she slowly puts on her black sweater*]: That's half of humanity disposed of.

TONY: All you're interested in is . . .

MILLY: I was under the impression that that night of love was your idea.

TONY: Love!

MILLY [*suddenly and for the first time hurt*]: You've made use of me, young Tony. You made use of me.

TONY [*guilty*]: Of course women are so much better than men.

MILLY [*grimly*]: Is that so?

TONY [*sentimental and shrill*]: You're so much stronger.

MILLY: That's very nice for you, isn't it?

TONY: But I mean it, you are.

MILLY: When I hear men saying that women are so much stronger than men, I feel like . . .

TONY: What?

MILLY: Reaching for my revolver.

TONY: I imagined it was a compliment.

MILLY: Did you now, love. I prefer the more obvious forms of contempt. [*she slowly puts on her black skirt*] If you really don't like sex why don't you leave us alone? Otherwise you're going to turn into one of those spiteful little men who spend their lives punishing women in bed . . . Where's my brooch? [*She adjusts the sweater, which last night was open over her shoulders, tight to her throat with a brooch.*]

TONY: Now you look like a respectable *Hausfrau*.

MILLY: You might also put in some time asking yourself why you have to say you don't like women.

TONY [*slowly sits up on the divan, legs crossed*]: Women, women, women . . . [*He meditatively and sensuously bites his own shoulder.*]

[MILLY *stands watching satirically, hands on hips.*]

MILLY: You might find it all more satisfactory if you took a mirror into bed with you.

TONY: I have no idea at all what you're talking about.

MILLY: Oh, I believe you. You probably don't.

TONY [*shrilly*]: You lay all last night in my arms. You were perfectly sweet. And now . . .

MILLY: What's the matter with you all, anyway? We've committed the basic and unforgivable crime of giving you birth – but we had no choice, after all . . . Well, God damn the lot of you. [*going towards door R*] I'm going home. For the sake of appearances.

TONY: Oh, don't worry about my reputation, please

MILLY [amazed]: Your reputation? [scornful] Your reputation. Why, do you consider yourself compromised? [laughs] I'm considering my Sandy.

TONY: Why? Your Sandy is such a man of the world.

MILLY: Not so far as I am concerned. I have preserved my Sandy's mental equilibrium by the practice of consummate hypocrisy. It is usually referred to as tact.

TONY: What a pity my mother thinks tact beneath her.

MILLY: It's always a mistake to treat you as if you were grownups. Always.

TONY [jumping up]: Milly, don't go. Don't go, Milly. [He goes after her.] You're not really going . . . I'm sorry if I hurt you.

MILLY [coming back, she stands with her hands on her hips, looking at him]: Young Tony, why don't you get out of here. For Christ's sake, get out.

TONY [sharply]: Mother told you to say that.

MILLY: The Lord help us. [Goes to him, puts her hands on his shoulders from behind. He leans his head back against her and closes his eyes.] You ought to get out, Tony. Bum around a bit. You can't stay here. Surely you can see that your mother's worried because you don't want any life of your own?

TONY: You mean, she wants a life of her own.

MILLY [exasperated]: Tony, you aren't ten years old.

TONY: What does she want? She wants to marry Uncle Mike? I don't believe it.

MILLY: Perhaps she thinks it would make you happy if she settled down.

TONY: With Uncle Mike? She's going to settle down with old Mike just to please me?

MILLY: But she's worried about you. You surely can see that she's bound to be worried about you?

TONY: With Aunty Mike. [laughs unpleasantly]

MILLY: And besides, she's lonely.

TONY: Lonely? My battling mum? Why on earth? She's never alone. [pause] Then if she's lonely, why does she want to get rid of me?

MILLY [dropping her hands, shrugs, and moves away]: I give up. I

simply give up. But you should get out. You're 22. You
should be banging and crashing around South America or
the Middle East, getting mixed up in all kinds of things,
making a fool of yourself, having women . . .

TONY [*wincing*]: Oh Christ!

MILLY: You ought to be shouting your head off about everything, revolutionizing, upsetting all the equilibriums.

TONY: Equilibrium? What equilibrium? You don't really
imagine that I should want to revolutionize after watching
your lot at it all my life? Upsetting the equilibrium . . . that's
just it! You're so childish . . . if there was, by any miracle,
an equilibrium anywhere you'd put a bomb under it just for
the sake of seeing everything rock. All I want is an equilibrium – just five minutes of stability. [*pause*] This house is
the only thing in my life that has – stayed in one place. It's
the only thing I can count on. Why should I want to leave
it? [MILLY *slowly comes up behind him again, cradles him against
her.*] I remember after our other house was blown up, that
night mother and I were lying under the bricks waiting to
be rescued, and my father was dead beside us, I remember
thinking that there would never be another house. I remember thinking mother would get killed too, and I'd have to
go to an orphanage. I remember lying there under the bricks
with the bombs falling . . . after that we were in one furnished
room after another for months and months. Then there was
this house. I remember the first few weeks we were here I
used to go secretly around looking at the walls, wondering
if the cracks were going to appear soon. I couldn't believe
a house could be something whole, without cracks. I love
this house. I don't want ever to leave it. I'd like to – pull it
over my ears like a pillow and never leave it.

MILLY: Tony, love, you can't build your life around a house.

TONY: Yes I can, yes I can . . . hold me, Milly.

MILLY [*rocking him*]: Tony, suppose you had to leave?

TONY [*eyes closed, blissfully, sleepily*]: Had to? Had to? Why?
No. I'll stay here always. Hold me, Milly.

MILLY: Tony, love, listen to me, I must talk to you.

TONY: No, don't talk. Just hold me.

MILLY: Tony, Tony, Tony. But I have to talk to you . . .

[MYRA *comes down the stairs, wearing her old trousers, without make-up, smoking.*]

MYRA: Good morning.

MILLY [*without letting* TONY *go*]: Good morning, Myra.

TONY [*from* MILLY'S *arms*]: Slept well, Mother?

MYRA: Thank you, no. [*to* MILLY, *smiling*] You're a very early visitor.

MILLY [*grinning*]: Not too early, I hope.

[*She lets her arms fall away from* TONY. TONY *moves away in a drifting listless movement to the window, leans there, back turned.* MYRA *raises her eyebrows at* MILLY. MILLY *gives a massive good-natured shrug.*]

TONY: More songs without words. Yes, Mother, the operation is successfully concluded.

MILLY: Do you want me to tidy up this bed again?

MYRA: I don't know, I haven't thought. I don't know what's going on, if Philip and Rosemary have made it up or not. If she's going home, then Tony can have his room back.

TONY [*turning*]: I wish someone would explain this to me — last night Rosemary was through with Uncle Philip. She hated and despised him. If she comes down those stairs announcing that the marriage is on, are you two wise women going to let her marry him? You both know quite well that she'll be miserable. [*They both shrug.*] What? You aren't going to say that you don't believe in interfering with other people's lives?

MYRA: What do you think we should do? Take her aside and warn her against Philip? How can we?

TONY: Why not?

MYRA: You should do it.

TONY: Why me?

MYRA: You're her age. She'll trust you.

TONY: Oh — hell. [*aggressively, to his mother*] Where's Sandy? Surely he should do it? He's the boy for public and personal relations.

MILLY: Tony dear, that girl likes you.

TONY [*amazed*]: She likes *me*?

MILLY [*patting him*]: You've been kind to her.

TONY: Oh.

MILLY [*kissing him*]: Bless you, dear boy.

MYRA [*watching them, ironically*]: Oh well, I don't know. I'm feeling very old this morning. [*goes to the mirror and looks at it*] Oh, oh, oh.

TONY: Then for heaven's sake put some lipstick on at least. [*She winces.*] Sorry. Sorry, Mother. [*goes to her and says with rough gentleness*] Mother, if you knew how I hate it, the way you go slopping around like this, you'd do something about it. Please.

MYRA [*touched by his tone, turning to him*]: Really? You really care? Well, I'll try.

TONY: You look so beautiful when you try.

MYRA: Why, Tony, I shall burst into tears.

TONY: Mother, you surely aren't going to marry old Mike?

MYRA: It would seem so.

TONY: You don't want to, do you?

MYRA: Would you hate it if I did?

TONY: But, Mother, he's an old man.

MYRA: [*touched to the point of tears*]: An old man . . . but Tony, I'm not far off 50 . . . [*laughing*] Oh, Tony, you are absurd. You're sweet. Well, of course I won't marry him if you don't like it.

TONY: Good God, how could I like it?

MYRA [*delighted*]: Well, that's easy, isn't it? [*She impulsively kisses him. He kisses her.*] Well, everything's all right, isn't it? [*Sits on the arm of a chair, humming 'Boohoo, you've got me crying for you'.*]

MILLY [*reprovingly*]: Poor Mike.

MYRA [*blissfully*]: Oh, I'm so happy, what a relief. I've been awake all night thinking of my gloriously exciting future.

TONY [*suddenly furious*]: You're as irresponsible as a child.

MYRA [*blissfully*]: Yes, I know, I know.

TONY [*shouting*]: You just pick people up and drop them.

MYRA: How could I pick up Mike and drop him? I've known him for a thousand years.

MILLY [*drily*]: Last night you said you'd marry him. Or didn't you?

TONY: It was announced, no doubt, to all your guests.

MYRA: Yes, it was. Yes. But he'll understand. Mike has always been so sweet.

TONY: Sweet. And there's Sandy. He's always sweet too. Where *is* Sandy?

MYRA: Oh, Sandy – well, I don't know.

TONY: You mean he wasn't sharing your insomnia last night?

MYRA [*coldly*]: Obviously not. I believe he went home.

MILLY: Oh, did he now? [MILLY *looks at* MYRA. MYRA *looks at* MILLY, *full of wild mischievous delight. She collapses in a chair, laughing.*]

MYRA: Oh, Milly, don't mind me – but this is one situation you can't walk out on.

[*As she laughs the door-bell rings, R.* TONY *looks out of window, turns to grin at* MILLY *and* MYRA. *Unwedges door.* SANDY *enters fast, goes straight to* MILLY.]

SANDY: Mother, you might have let me know that you had plans to stay out last night.

MILLY: I might have done. If I'd had plans.

SANDY: I was worried about you.

MILLY: I never worry about you. I know you can look after yourself.

SANDY: Where were you?

MILLY: Here.

SANDY [*relieved*]: Oh, you were with Myra. Oh . . . [*looks at* TONY *and stiffens*] I see.

[MYRA *laughs.* SANDY *turns on her, furious.*]

MYRA: Sandy dear, have you been worrying about *me* all this time and I never knew it?

SANDY [*furious*]: Really, Myra, I would never have believed it possible that you could behave in such sheer bad taste, really Myra . . .

[MYRA *laughs. Her attention is caught by* ROSEMARY *and* PHILIP *at the top of the stairs.* SANDY *turns, then* MILLY *and* TONY. *They all stand and watch as* ROSEMARY *and* PHILIP *slowly descend.*]

ROSEMARY [*half-way down the stairs, in command of the situation, bravely making a necessary announcement*]: Good morning. Philip and I have talked it over and we have decided that it would be very much more sensible *not* to get married. [*No one knows what to say.*]

TONY: I'm delighted there is one sensible person in this house.

[ROSEMARY *leaves* PHILIP *at the foot of the stairs and goes to stand by* TONY *at the window. The stage is now like this:* TONY *and* ROSEMARY *standing side by side, back to the window, watching.* PHILIP *at foot of the stairs.* SANDY *and* MILLY *together near the door, R.* MYRA *by herself at centre.*]

PHILIP: Well, Myra, I'm sorry all this has been foisted on you.
MYRA: Oh, don't mention it [*smiles ironically at him. Her smile brings him across to her*]

[THEY *are now close together, looking into each other's face.*]

SANDY [*from beside* MILLY]: Philip, perhaps I could go down to the office with you . . .

[*He is about to go over to* PHILIP: MILLY *grabs him by the arm and makes him stay by her. She keeps tight hold of him.*]

PHILIP [*to* MYRA, *in a low voice*]: So everyone's back where they started – except you? You're going to marry old Mike?
MYRA: No.
PHILIP: Well, old girl?
MYRA [*with grim humour*]: My hair isn't grey yet . . . I wouldn't forgive you, Philip. I wouldn't be the good woman sitting on the mountain-top forgiving you your sins.
PHILIP: Oh Lord, Myra, I'm tired . . . I really would like something – quiet. [*drily, tender, bitter*] Well, Myra?
MYRA: I've told you, I wouldn't forgive you. You cast me in the one role long enough – now you want me to be the

quiet woman waiting to welcome you home? But I wouldn't forgive you. If I did it would be contempt. *I've* never despised you, Philip.

PHILIP [*half-groaning*]: Oh, Lord, it is utterly *intolerable.*

MYRA [*half-groaning turning away*]: Oh God, yes . . .

SANDY: Philip, if you're going to the office, we could go together.

PHILIP [*impatiently*]: Yes.

MILLY [*holding* SANDY]: I was under the impression you came here for me – why are you so interested in Philip all of a sudden. [TONY *suddenly laughs.*] Oh, I see . . . I thought that was the job Philip had arranged for Tony.

SANDY: But I thought Tony had turned it down unconditionally.

TONY: He has, don't worry.

SANDY: I wouldn't have dreamed of approaching Philip unless I was sure Tony wasn't interested.

PHILIP: I'm late. I must go.

MILLY [*holding* SANDY *fast*]: You come home. You can arrange your career with Philip another day.

PHILIP: Where's my briefcase?

SANDY [*turning furiously on* MILLY]: Mother, if you didn't want me to get a decent job and do all the regular things why did you set me up for it?

MILLY: Oh – no one'll ever blame you for anything!

SANDY [*furious*]: Well, why did you? What am I doing wrong?

MILLY: Of course it's my fault. I'm your mother – that's what I'm for.

SANDY: And if Tony wants the job I'll stand down. What do you expect me to do? Be a tramp, like Tony?

MYRA [*absolutely delighted*]: Why, Tony darling, why didn't you tell me.

TONY: Oh, my God!

ROSEMARY [*holding* TONY]: Shhh, Tony.

MYRA: Why, darling Tony, that's wonderful, it would be so *good* for you.

PHILIP [*exasperated*]: Really, Myra, how can you be such a romantic.

TONY [*breaking from* ROSEMARY, *standing beside* PHILIP, *accusing her*]: Mother, why should it be *good* for me?

MYRA [*at the two of them*]: What have I done now? If you want to be a tramp, am I expected to lock you in the house?

TONY ⎱ [*together*,              Mother . . .
PHILIP ⎰ *shouting at her*]:    Myra, you're utterly intolerable!

MYRA [*gaily*]: What's wrong? Perhaps I'll be a tramp, too: why not?

TONY [*shouting at her*]: You are a tramp!

[MIKE *has entered*, R, *carrying a bunch of flowers*. PHILIP, TONY, *and* MYRA *have not seen him*.]

MILLY: Myra, you have a visitor.

[MYRA *turns*, PHILIP *and* TONY *fall back*.]

MIKE: Myra darling, I know it's appallingly early, but I had to come. [*He holds out the flowers. She does not take them.*] I've had some really lovely news, darling. Or, at least, I do hope you'll think so. I'm invited to China. For a series of lectures. And I spoke to the organizer this morning. If we're married, of course you'll come too. It would be a rather lovely honeymoon.

MYRA: I'm sorry, Mike.

MIKE: But, of course, if you feel you don't want to leave your committee work now I'll quite understand.

MYRA: Mike, I'm sorry. Last night I was just . . . [MIKE *stares at her, helpless.*] I'm so sorry. We'll just have to go on as we've always done. You must forgive me. You've forgiven me often enough, haven't you?

[MIKE *seems as if he's crumpling inwardly. He stares at her, around at the others, then blunders out*, R, *still holding the flowers*.]

TONY: Oh, *Mother!* [*He turns to watch out of window.*]

MYRA: Oh, that was bad, that was very bad.

MILLY: Yes, love, it was. Very bad.

PHILIP [*furious*]: Myra, you are utterly intolerable. [MYRA *lays her head down on the back of her chair.*] Intolerable. I'm very late. [*he is on his way out* R, *remembering* ROSEMARY] Good-bye,

Rosemary. [at door, back to MYRA] I'll be seeing you, Myra
Look after yourself.

[ROSEMARY *has not responded to* PHILIP's *good-bye. But she stands at the window, beside* TONY, *watching him go.*]

SANDY [*escaping from* MILLY]: I'll go with Philip. [*from door, hastily*] Good-bye, Myra. I'll be seeing you.

MYRA [*who has not lifted her head from the chair-back*]: Oh damn, damn, damn.

MILLY [*to* MYRA]: Charming. All quite charming. Oh well, look after yourself, love. And don't forget that tape-recording for the meeting. We'll need it. Meet you in the pub as usual. [*goes out R*].

TONY [*turning from window*]: Mother, why did you do that?

MYRA: I thought you wanted me to.

TONY: Mother, he's standing in the garden, crying. He's standing there, crying. Did you have to do it like that? Oh, damn it all, Mother.

MYRA: I've broken with Mike. After twenty years.

TONY: Yes, and how did you do it? As if he were . . .

MYRA: And I've broken finally with Philip. That's all finished. And I've broken with Sandy. Well? Isn't that what you wanted?

TONY: I don't want you to do anything you don't . . . [MYRA *laughs.*] I don't want . . . All I want is to be here in this house, with you, Mother – and some sort of . . . dignity. I'm so tired of all the brave speeches and the epic battles and the gestures. Wouldn't it be enough if we were just peaceful together? This house is like a sounding-board.

MYRA: Yes, I was thinking – we should move to a flat. This house is much too big.

TONY [*appalled*]: Mother, you can't be serious.

MYRA [*evasively*]: You don't think so? Why not?

TONY: Oh no, no, no.

MYRA: But it's so big. And I've got a bit of money. We could get ourselves a nice flat.

TONY: Money, yes. Where did you get it from?

MYRA [*proudly*]: Five hundred pounds. And more later.

TONY: Five hundred pounds. But where? We've never had all that money all at once.

MYRA: Oh, money from heaven. [*She moves away to escape his questioning, notices* ROSEMARY, *still bent by the window, back turned to them. She goes to* ROSEMARY *and puts her arm around her.*] Don't cry, Rosemary. [*She turns* ROSEMARY *round and smiles at her.*]

ROSEMARY [*rather bitterly, smiling back*]: I'm not crying.

TONY [*desperately anxious, pulling* MYRA *away from* ROSEMARY]: Mother, I want to know. You're not just going to get out of it like that.

MYRA: Tony, before you settle down to being an honest electrician, I wish you'd take that money and . . .

TONY: What? Sow a few wild oats?

MYRA: Oh . . . sow anything you damned well please.

TONY: Mother, I'm being serious. In about a month from now I'm going to get myself a job. As an electrician. It's what I want. Work for eight hours a day, regularly paid, three square meals a day and . . .

MYRA [*derisively*]: Security! [*to* ROSEMARY] All he wants is security.

ROSEMARY: But Myra, what's wrong with that?

MYRA [*shrugging contemptuously*]: Oh, I don't know . . . I suppose you'll spend jolly evenings in the local coffee bar, join a skiffle group, become a scruffy little bohemian, one of the neo-conformists, enjoying all the postures of rebellion from safe positions of utter respectability.

TONY: That's it, exactly.

MYRA: 'And thus from no heights canst thou fall.'

TONY [*derisively, to* ROSEMARY]: Heights, she wants. [*derisively, at* MYRA] Heights, heights . . . We'll leave you to skip about on the heights. Mother, why don't you leave people alone? Just leave us alone . . . do you know what I'd really enjoy doing? I'd like to paint this house. To decorate it. I really would.

MYRA: You want to decorate the house? [*to* ROSEMARY, *blankly*] He's 22 and he wants to spend his time decorating the house.

ROSEMARY: I don't see what's wrong with it.

MYRA [to TONY]: Wait a bit, don't start painting the house yet.

TONY: But why should I wait? I'll go out this afternoon and choose colours. It'll be fun. [suspiciously] What's up? What are you up to?

MYRA: Oh, nothing. Nothing. Look, I've got an awful lot to do this morning. Will you help me? It's that tape-recording. Sandy said he'd help me but now he's gone.

TONY: Oh, no.

MYRA: But I promised it for the meeting tonight.

TONY: Meetings, meetings. Who cares what's said at meetings.

MYRA: Tony, if you're trying to stop my work for the committee I'm not going to.

TONY: All these people in and out. All the noise, the speeches, the mess.

MYRA: I'm not going to become a sort of monument to your desire for – whatever it is.

TONY: Dignity.

MYRA: If you call dignity sitting with your hands folded waiting to be blown up – well, I'm not going to be blackmailed into inertia. Please help me. Are you an electrician or are you not? I want you to play that tape back and take out the bits that are simply dull.

TONY: Dull!

MYRA: Will you or won't you? If not I'll ring up . . .

TONY: Who? Uncle Mike?

MYRA: It seems at the moment there's no one I can ring up. At least, not with dignity. [She suddenly bursts into tears, and turns away.]

TONY [appalled]: Mother.

MYRA: Oh, leave me alone [goes to window, stands with her back turned].

[ROSEMARY takes his arm, shakes her head. Indicates the machine.]

TONY: Oh, all right, I'll do it.

ROSEMARY: I'll help you.

[*The two crouch by the machine.* TONY *starts it going. After a few seconds of war noises, shuts it off.*]

TONY: Oh Lord, *no*.

MYRA [*still with back turned, her voice almost in control*]: You see, people have no imagination. That's the trouble.

TONY [*to her back*]: Can't you see that people can't bear to think about it? It's all too big for everyone. They simply can't bear to think about it. [*as* ROSEMARY *shakes her head at him*] Oh, all *right*.

MYRA: There's some new tape there if you want it.

TONY [*putting on the new tape; begins to run it*]: There, that's better.

ROSEMARY: What are you doing?

TONY: Playing a record of silence.

MYRA [*still with back turned*]: Tony, you said you'd help me.

TONY: A clean sheet. A new page. Rosemary, say something very simple, very quiet, very beautiful, something I'd like to hear when I play this thing back.

ROSEMARY [*in an urgent whisper*]: Tony, your mother is *crying*.

TONY: But what can I do? . . . Say something, Rosemary, do say something.

ROSEMARY: But what?

TONY: Surely there's something you need to say.

ROSEMARY: But what about?

TONY: Anything. What you feel about — life.

ROSEMARY: But I don't know.

TONY: Then — people.

ROSEMARY: Who?

TONY: Anybody.

ROSEMARY: Why?

TONY: Oh Lord. [*He switches off machine.*] All right, let's have bombs and blasts and gunfire. Oh *Lord*. For instance, you've just decided not to marry Philip. Well *you're* not going to cry, are you?

ROSEMARY: I've finished crying.

[MYRA *turns round from the window. She has controlled herself. Stands watching ironically.*]

TONY: Are you unhappy?

ROSEMARY: Yes.

TONY: But you wouldn't have been happy with him, would you?

ROSEMARY [*turning and seeing* MYRA]: Well . . .

MYRA: Go on.

ROSEMARY: I don't think I expected to be.

TONY: Then why did you say you'd marry him?

ROSEMARY: He said . . . people should be ready to take chances. He said people shouldn't be afraid.

TONY: And so you said you'd marry him?

[ROSEMARY *turns, gives* MYRA *another troubled but defiant look.* MYRA *nods at her to proceed.*]

ROSEMARY: Yes. Philip suddenly came into my life and made fun of everything I did. He said I wasn't alive at all. He made me read books.

TONY [*laughing*]: Books!

ROSEMARY: Yes, he said I might just as well be dead, the way I was living. He said when I came to die I wouldn't know I'd ever been alive . . .

TONY: And that's why you said you'd marry him?

ROSEMARY [*after another look at* MYRA, *who meets it with a grave ironical nod*]: Yes. He said there was only one thing people should be afraid of – of not growing. He said happiness didn't matter. People should grow, be everything, do a lot of things, and never be afraid of being unhappy . . .

TONY [*laughing derisively*]: Philip said all that, did he? Uncle Philip did? Well, look at him now, look at him now . . .

ROSEMARY [*suddenly furious, leaping up and away from him*]: Yes, he did. And I won't have you saying things about Philip, I won't have you . . . [*She begins to cry and* MYRA *comes up and puts her arms around her from behind.*]

MYRA: There, darling. It's all right.

TONY [*shouting*]: Oh yes, that's very much your cup of tea, isn't it, Mother? You like that, don't you? Suffering – the great cult of suffering. Strength through pain . . . that's your creed.

MYRA: Oh, shut up and stop bullying people.

TONY [*shouting*]: Well, I don't want any of it – I tell you, pain doesn't exist. I refuse to feel it . . .

MYRA [*to* ROSEMARY]: There . . . Listen – you don't regret having known Philip, do you?

ROSEMARY: Oh *no*.

MYRA: Then that's all. [*She makes* ROSEMARY *lift her face: she smiles into it.*] There, that's better. It's all not so serious – is it?

TONY: What are you doing now? Dancing on another emotional grave.

MYRA: Oh Tony . . . [*She leaves* ROSEMARY *and comes to* TONY.] I've got to tell you something. No, listen. I've been screwing up my courage to tell you.

TONY [*already half-knows*]: No – *what*?

MYRA [*after a pause, while she screws herself up to tell him*]: Tony . . . I've sold the house.

[*There is a long silence.*]

TONY [*very quiet, almost in a whisper*]: You've sold the house. Oh, my God, you've sold the house. [*grabbing at* ROSEMARY, *shaking her as if she were* MYRA] My God, she's sold the house!

ROSEMARY: But Tony, only yesterday you were talking about being a tramp.

TONY [*after a pause, as the word tramp strikes him*]: Tramp? A tramp? . . . [*He is almost doubled up with pain.*] She's sold it. And do you know why? To raise five hundred pounds so that I can go and sow my wild oats. Oh God, God. So that I can go bumming off and having love affairs and revolutionizing . . . [*He cackles with hysterical laughter.*]

ROSEMARY: Tony, don't do that. Stop it.

MYRA: Leave him. [*She slumps down in a chair, in the pose she had before, head down against the back of it.*]

TONY: My God, my mother's done that to me. She's done that to me. She's my mother and she might just as well have taken a knife and stabbed me with it. She's my mother and she knows so little about me that she doesn't suspect that there's one thing I love in this world, and it's this house . . .

ROSEMARY: Tony, stop it, stop it, stop it.

TONY [*pulling himself away from* ROSEMARY, *shouting at* MYRA'S *head — she is sitting rocking back and forth with the pain of it*]: God, but you're destructive, destructive, destructive. There isn't anything you touch which doesn't go to pieces. You just go on from mess to mess . . . you live in a mess of love affairs and committees and . . . you live in a mess like a *pig*, Mother . . . you're all over everything like a great crawling spider . . .

ROSEMARY [*forcibly pulling him away*]: Tony, stop it at once.

TONY [*hundred up in* ROSEMARY'S *grasp*]: Sometimes when I hear her come down the stairs I feel every nerve in my body shrieking. I can't stand her, I simply can't stand her . . . [*He collapses into chair, goes completely limp.* ROSEMARY *goes to* MYRA, *is too afraid of her clenched-up pose of pain to touch her, stands helplessly looking from one to the other.*]

TONY [*limply*]: Now we'll have to leave here and live in some-damned pretty little flat somewhere. I can't bear it, I can't bear it . . .

[*There is a silence.* MYRA *slowly straightens herself, stands up, walks slowly across the room.* ROSEMARY *watches her fearfully.*]

MYRA: If you hate me as much as that why do you put so much energy into getting me alone with you into this house. Well, why? For the pleasure of torturing me? Or of being tortured?

ROSEMARY: Oh Myra, he didn't mean it.

MYRA [*with a short laugh*]: Perhaps he does mean it. There's no law that says a son must like his mother, is there? [*after a pause*] And vice versa. [*She lights a cigarette. It can be seen her hand is trembling violently. Otherwise she is calm. Almost limp, with the same limpness as* TONY'S.]

TONY [*looking at her, he begins to understand what he has done. Almost apologetically*]: I can't think why one of you doesn't say: There are millions of people in the world living in mud huts, and you make this fuss about moving from one comfortable home to another. Isn't that what I'm supposed to be feeling?

MYRA: Since you've said it, there's no need for me to.

TONY [*almost querulous*]: The other thing you could say is: Wait until you've got to my age and see if you've done any better. Well – if I haven't done any better I'd have the grace to kill myself.

MYRA: Luckily I don't take myself so seriously. Well, I'm going to leave you to it.

TONY [*desperately anxious*]: What do you mean, where are you going?

MYRA: I don't know.

TONY: You're not going?

MYRA: Why not? I don't propose to live with someone who can't *stand* me. Why should I ... [*She makes a movement as if expanding, or about to take flight.*] It just occurs to me that for the first time in my life I'm free.

TONY: Mother, where are you going?

MYRA: It occurs to me that for the last twenty-two years my life has been governed by yours – by your needs. Oh, you may not think so – but the way I've lived, what I've done, my whole life has been governed by your needs. And what for ... [*contemptuously*] What for – a little monster of egotism – that's what you are. A petty, envious, spiteful little egotist, concerned with nothing but yourself.

ROSEMARY [*almost in tears*]: Oh Myra, stop, stop.

MYRA [*ignoring her, to* TONY]: Well, I'm sure it's my fault. Obviously it is. If I've spent half my life bringing you up and you turn out – as you have – then it's my life that's a failure, isn't it? Well, it's not going to be a failure in future.

TONY: Mother, what are you going to do?

MYRA: There are a lot of things I've wanted to do for a long time, and I haven't done them. [*laughing*] Perhaps I'll take the money and go off; why not? Or perhaps I'll be a tramp. I could be, you know. I could walk out of this house with my needs in a small suitcase ... and I shall. Or perhaps I'll go on that boat to the Pacific to the testing area – I wanted to do that and didn't, because of you.

TONY: Mother, you might get killed.

MYRA: Dear me, I might get killed. And what of it? I don't propose to keep my life clutched in my hand like small change . . .

TONY: Mother, you can't just walk off into – *nothing*.

MYRA: Nothing? I don't have to shelter under a heap of old bricks – like a frightened mouse. I'm going. I'll come back and collect what I need when I've decided what I'm going to do [*goes towards door R*].

TONY [*angry and frightened*]: Mother.

[*She turns at the door. She is quite calm, but she is crying.*]

Mother, you're crying.

MYRA [*laughing*]: Why not? I'm nearly 50 – and it's true there's nothing much to show for it. Except that I've never been afraid to take chances and make mistakes. I've never wanted security and safety and the walls of respectability – you damned little petty-bourgeois. My God, the irony of it – that *we* should have given birth to a generation of little office boys and clerks and . . . little people who count their pensions before they're out of school . . . little petty-bourgeois. Yes, I am crying. I've been alive for fifty years. Isn't that good enough cause for tears . . . [*she goes out R*].

TONY [*amazed, not believing it*]: But Rosemary, she's gone.

ROSEMARY: Yes.

TONY: But she'll come back.

ROSEMARY: No, I don't think so. [*She comes to him, puts her arm around him. They crouch down, side by side, arms around each other.*]

TONY: Rosemary, do you know that not one word of what she said made any sense to me at all . . . slogans, slogans, slogans . . .

ROSEMARY: What's the matter with being safe – and ordinary. What's wrong with being ordinary – and safe?

TONY: Rosemary, listen – never in the whole history of the world have people made a battle-cry out of being ordinary. Never. Supposing we all said to the politicians – we refuse to be heroic. We refuse to be brave. We are bored with all the noble gestures – what then, Rosemary?

ROSEMARY: Yes. Ordinary and safe.
TONY: Leave us alone, we'll say. Leave us alone to live. Just
leave us alone . . .

CURTAIN